OUR GOD

Attributes of God

Russell G. Jones

ACCENT BOOKS
Denver, Colorado

ACCENT BOOKS

A division of Accent Publications, Inc.
12100 W. Sixth Avenue
P.O. Box 15337
Denver, Colorado 80215

Library of Congress Catalog Card Number 80-66135

ISBN 0-89636-069-5

Second Printing

This book is dedicated to my wife, Ruth, who will receive most of the reward if these studies prove to be useful in the plan and purpose of God. She encouraged me to prepare the studies for publication; she took time from her own writing schedule to type the material for submission and she has encouraged me along the way to finish the project.

Contents

Introduction

Scripture clearly teaches that the Christian represents God to the world. Why is it then that few Christians really know what God is like? How can they represent someone about whom they know so little?

It is important that we as a people of God understand Him. Yet, current religious magazines and theological journals emphasize the fact that we really do not know very much about God.

The Bible tells us we are to be conformed to the image of Christ so that we can manifest the nature of God as we live day by day. It is impossible to give any real indication of the kind of God we claim to know and serve unless we know His character. How can we say we reflect the nature of our God when we really do not understand His nature? Part of the problem is that we think it is impossible to understand God. After all, if He is God, we reason, obviously we cannot understand everything about Him. This is true, of course. There are aspects of God which are incomprehensible. However, this does not mean that we cannot come to some knowledge of Him.

If we, as sinful, finite, human beings, were to depend upon our own ability to understand Him, it would be a complete impossibility. But God has revealed Himself to us. Through a study of His Word, we can come to a knowledge of God. Although, with our limited understanding, in this life we can never come to a complete understanding of the infinite God, we need to know something about Him.

Theologians divide the attributes of God in various ways. In this study I will not attempt to categorize or list them. You can find lists in your own theology books if you are interested. I will simply discuss the various attributes and make practical application to our lives.

If you would like to study the attributes in depth, I suggest you use the concordance in the back of your Bible and look under "attributes of God." If you use a separate concordance, you must look for the words that are used to convey the thought. In the case of *immutability*, you would look up *change* or *variable*. Whichever you use, you will find many passages in both the Old and New Testaments which prove or illustrate God's characteristics.

Perhaps the term *attribute* is not a good label for the characteristics of God which we will be discussing. The use of that word may imply that an attribute is something that is added to God. In his book, *The Knowledge of the Holy*, A. W. Tozer says that an attribute is anything that God has revealed about Himself. Some theologians do not talk about the attributes of God. They discuss His properties, perfections or virtues. Whatever name they use, they are referring to the things we will consider: His immutability, His holiness, His justice and His other characteristics.

Attributes are simply the perfections which are true of God as set forth in Scripture and are visibly used by Him in works of creation, providence and redemption. In studying the various attributes of God, I will discuss three areas. First, I will try to show how the Scripture itself or God's works establish the fact that He has a specific quality.

Second, I will discuss how God demonstrates that attribute. We can see many of the virtues in His creative activity. He also demonstrates many of His attributes in His providence and the care of the things He has created. He reveals almost all of His attributes in the work of redemption.

Third, I will show how the attribute should affect the Christian's life.

If God had not revealed Himself, we really could not understand these attributes. We can learn certain things about God without direct revelation, but very little. As a matter of fact, if we accept natural revelation, that is, that God reveals Himself in nature, there is nothing we can learn without God's revelation. Apart from these two areas, we would have no sources of knowledge about God at all. We get our basic information about God from Scripture or as He is seen in the works of creation, providence and redemption.

Tozer lists twenty attributes in *The Knowledge of the Holy*. In his book, *Gleanings in the Godhead*, Arthur W. Pink lists twenty-five but they are not the same as Tozer's list. Some are the same virtues but are given a slightly different name. I have chosen to study fifteen.

Because we are finite beings and He is infinite, God cannot fully reveal Himself to us. However, we know from Scripture that some day we will know Him, fully know Him. The Scripture says, "Now are we the sons of God, and it doth not yet appear what we shall be: but we know that, when he shall appear, we shall be like him; for we shall see him as he is" (I John 3:2).

This implies that our knowledge of God will be the same as His. Another passage says that "we shall know as we are known." Here the one knowing us is God, and so we will be able to know God as He knows us. In the glorified state, we will comprehend God fully. Nevertheless, even though God is incomprehensible in this life, God has revealed Himself to us and to that extent we may know Him now. It is the Christian's responsibility to come to the knowledge of God. There is no excuse for our not knowing Him as fully as He has revealed Himself. I encourage you to study the Word God has given us. Through study we can come to a knowledge of Him.

We can also see His attributes in the world which He created and controls. Although they are not fully revealed here, we certainly can see evidence of His nature. By studying His Word and observing how these attributes, virtues or perfections are utilized in the creation and control of the world, we can come to a more intimate, deeper knowledge of our God.

Because God saves sinners through faith in the person and work of the Lord Jesus Christ, He expects redeemed sinners to grow to be like Himself. Romans 8 tells us that we are predestined to be conformed to the image of His Son. Since Jesus Christ is fully God, we are to be exactly like God. If we are to be like God, we must know Him. We must have an understanding of His perfections and His virtues. The things listed as fruit of the Spirit in Galatians 5:22,23 are nothing more nor less than the attributes of God. We are to show love; we are to be long-suffering; we are to be kind.

By revealing these characteristics in our lives, we demonstrate the attributes of God. In this way, we are to make God known to others—not merely through what we say but what we are.

It is my prayer that as a result of these studies you will come to a deeper understanding of our God and that you not only will know more about Him, but that you will become like Him.

You see, it is not merely enough to know about God. We must have fellowship with God. We must spend time with Him. We must meditate upon Him. We must worship Him. As we do this, the very image of God will be manifested in us.

What does it mean to have a God who is immutable; a God who is good; a God who is holy and just; a God who has all knowledge and wisdom; a God who is patient, loving and merciful; a God who is truth; a God who is a God of wrath and of jealousy? Do you manifest any of these things in your life?

1. His Immutability

The immutability of God, or His changelessness, is basic to any understanding of God. It is also basic to our daily living. The world is in a state of flux or change. The only absolute many accept today is that there are no absolutes; everything changes. In a society which is based upon this philosophy, Christians need something that is unchangeable. We find this in our God.

Some years ago when our children were younger, school officials invited parents to come in and talk to them about an accelerated program of mathematics which was being introduced into the curriculum. Our daughter, Judith, was placed in the pilot program. By the time she was in junior high school, she was taking high school math. I talked to the teacher about this.

"Now, what is this going to do for her?" I asked. "Will this meet her requirements when she gets into high school?"

"Oh, yes, no problem!"

Of course, you can guess what happened. By the time she got into high school, the whole approach to teaching math had changed. I had to go in and argue with the officials to convince them she had taken the required math when she was still in junior high. In merely a few years the approach to teaching math had changed twice.

This is true not only in the area of math, but it is also true in the area of science. We tend to think science is the most unchangeable of subjects. Yet, this is not necessarily true. When I took science in college, light was considered to be waves, but that concept has changed.

I have a son-in-law who majored in physics. "What is light?" I asked him one day.

"It depends," he told me.

"What do you mean 'it depends'?"

"Well," he said, "it depends on what you want to explain."

"I want to explain light," I told him.

"Well, it depends."

"Tell me, what does it depend on?"

"If you're explaining some phenomena and need to explain light in terms of waves, you do so," he told me.

"I always thought light was a wave."

"It depends."

"What else can light be?" I asked.

"It can be explained as particles."

"Why do you explain it as particles?"

"Well, it depends on what you are explaining," he said. "If the explanation demands that light be particles, you explain it as particles."

"So what is it?" I persisted. "Is it waves or particles?"

"It depends," he replied.

14

"Thanks," I told him and gave up. I did not want to argue with my son-in-law.

I read recently it is no longer certain that Newton's law of gravity is correct. Philosophers and even some theologians say concepts and ideas change from day to day and we cannot be absolutely certain what we should believe. In the midst of such a changing society we need something that does not change.

According to the Scriptures, that is our God. He is immutable. What does it mean when we say God is immutable? We are saying God is unchangeable in His essence, His nature and His perfection. There is no change in God. He remains always the same. We say God is omniscient; that is, He is all-knowing. When we apply the attribute of immutability to His knowledge, we say God cannot gain in knowledge, nor can He lose knowledge. God always remains the same. When we look at the immutability of God with respect to time, we say He is eternal because eternity looks at duration. God does not change with respect to time. He always is. When we talk about immutability, we are looking at the state of God. He continues to exist in the same way. In order to see its full value, we need to consider the immutability of God with all His other attributes. However, it is difficult for us to comprehend immutability because we all change.

A few years ago a man with whom I had attended seminary dropped into my office. I had not seen him since our seminary days.

"Guess who I saw today?" I asked my wife when

I got home that evening. When she couldn't guess, I told her. "You know, he's an old man!"

"Isn't he the same age as you?" my wife asked.

I was silent for a minute then slowly said, "I guess he is, but he has aged far more than I."

He appeared to have changed so much because I had not seen him for twenty years. You see, I look at myself in the mirror every morning when I shave. Every time I comb my hair or wash my face, I see myself in the mirror. I have changed, but I have changed so gradually that I have not noticed how much. I am sure my friend went home and told his wife, "My! You ought to see that Jones. He's an old man!"

We are used to change and therefore we think everything changes. God, however, does not change.

In what respect is God unchangeable? God does not change in His essence. There is no alteration to His substance. He always remains the same. If this were not true, God could not have said, "I am that I am," in response to Moses who asked, "Whom shall I say hath sent me?" (Exodus 3:14). God's answer indicated there is no change in Him. There is no past. There is no future.

If God could change in other attributes, His immutability would not be true. However, God does not change in His other attributes. God's knowledge remains the same. He does not gain in knowledge; He does not lose knowledge. This seems somewhat unusual because we are especially good at losing knowledge.

God, on the other hand, can limit His knowledge.

In that sense He can say He no longer remembers our sin. That is an act of the will and not a denial of His immutability. There is no change in God's will or purpose. His plan always remains the same. There is no change in God as far as His place is concerned because He is omnipresent. He is everywhere. He *cannot* change as far as His place is concerned. His time always remains the same: no past, no present, no future. He is always the same.

Is there proof God is immutable? We can prove it from Scripture. "I said, O my God, take me not away in the midst of my days; thy years are throughout all generations. Of old hast thou laid the foundation of the earth: and the heavens are the work of thy hands. They shall perish, but thou shalt endure: yea, all of them shall wax [become] old like a garment; as a vesture shalt thou change them, and they shall be changed: But thou art the same, and thy years shall have no end" (Psalm 102:24-27).

Consider also Isaiah 46:9-10: "Remember the former things of old: for I am God, and there is none else; I am God, and there is none like me. Declaring the end from the beginning, and from ancient times the things that are not yet done, saying, My counsel shall stand, and I will do all my pleasure."

Malachi 3:6 confirms this as well. "For I am the Lord, I change not; therefore ye sons of Jacob are not consumed."

James 1:17 says, "Every good gift and every perfect gift is from above, and cometh down from the Father of lights, with whom is no variableness, neither shadow of turning.''

These are just four of the many passages of Scripture that clearly indicate our God is unchangeable. This is the kind of God we need in a changing society such as the one in which we live. When all concepts of knowledge are changing, when customs are changing; in the midst of this fluid situation, we need an unchangeable God.

Yet, can God be considered immutable if He created? Does the fact that God created the universe, the world and man indicate He is not truly immutable? Actually, when we stop to think about this, God's creativity does not mean there is any real change in His *essence* or *being*. It is true He can now have fellowship with others but that does not mean He has changed. The fact that He created does not prove He is changeable. It simply proves He has the ability, the power, to create. This was according to His will. You see, since we do not know what God's will is in detail, we cannot say God's will changed when He created. All we can say is, since God did create, it must be in accordance with His will. There is no change in His will. Creation, then, does not prove God actually changed.

Did God change when Jesus Christ, the second person of the Godhead, became incarnate? Could God become a man and still be immutable? Again, this does not really prove the immutability of God is a false concept. The fact, that Jesus Christ, the eternal Son of God, took upon Himself a human form does not mean He is no longer God. He still is exactly the same in His essence as before the incarnation.

18

The addition of humanity to Christ does not make any change in His eternal being. He still is eternal. He still is truly God.

It *does* make a change as far as the use of one of His attributes is concerned. The Lord Jesus Christ can no longer be omnipresent because He is limited by a physical body, but there is no real change in the essence of God. The fact that the use of one attribute changes does not deny the immutability of Christ, the second person of the Godhead. God can limit His use of any of His attributes. Jesus Christ did this when He became incarnate.

Scripture says God repents. Does this mean God has a change of mind? God's repentance does not prove He has changed in His inner being. Actually, it means God simply changed His response because of the actions of men. God, as the Creator, made man. When a man responds to God in certain ways, God in turn responds differently from what He might have if the actions of His creature had been different. This does not indicate any change in His purpose or will. He simply responds to what His creature does. The fact that God sometimes repents does not necessarily imply an essential change in the nature of God Himself.

Does unfulfilled prophecy indicate a change in God? No, this does not disprove the immutability of God. Rather, it simply means God has made some prophecies conditional. If the conditions are not met, the prophecies are not fulfilled. When the conditions are met, any conditional prophecy, of course, is fulfilled. There are many unconditional prophecies in Scripture and these are fulfilled whether or not man responds as he ought. However, leaving some prophecy unfulfilled does not mean any change in the will of God or in His essential being.

The change from love to displeasure or from displeasure to love does not mean God has changed in His basic essence. He still remains the same. God loves me with an everlasting love because I am in Jesus Christ. The fact that I may sin and thus lead Him to judge me does not mean His love has changed toward me. It is true, God responds differently because of my actions. This, however, does not mean a change in God Himself. It merely means a change in God's attitude toward me.

Does God change when He changes His methods of dealing with men? In the Old Testament God gave the people of Israel the Law of Moses and His actions with them were set in a framework of legality. On the other hand, since the death and resurrection of Christ, God has dealt with humans within a framework of grace. This, however, does not mean a change in His essence. He is perfectly free to change His dealings with men if He so desires.

What should the immutability of God mean to us? We ought to recognize that such a God is worthy of our worship. The very fact that He is unchangeable means that if we meet the requirements He has established for fellowship, He must accept us.

Our consideration of God's immutability should make us aware of how different we are. Scripture tells us that we are to be like God. We should not be "blown about by every wind of doctrine." Hebrews 13:8 says, "Jesus Christ, the same yesterday, and to day, and for ever." Jesus remains the same; therefore, our beliefs about Him should remain the same. We need not continually change our doctrinal position. God's immutability should cause us to be like Him. We should pray that God will make us men and women who are firm in our convictions. We should know what we believe and should stand for it. Our very natures are built upon the nature of God.

God does not change, but we change. We change what we like to eat. We change the way we dress. We change the style of our hair. We do all kinds of things which are different. God, however, always remains the same. Certainly, we can change these outward things, but when it comes to our being we ought to be immutable, as God is. We should not change in the very essence of our nature. If we are truly children of God we should give evidence of the immutability of our God. People ought to be able to depend on us. Particularly, people ought to be able to depend on us as children of God.

The immutability of God should comfort us. We know God's Word will be fulfilled. God's Word cannot be changed. When God says He will do something for us on the basis of Jesus Christ, He will. When God tells us He will give us the help we need in time of trouble, He will give it to us. When God says He will not let us be tempted above that which we are able, He will not allow more temptation than we can endure. We should be fully aware

God cannot change His Word and therefore, He will do what He has promised.

Furthermore, God's immutability should encourage us to pray. Since God does not change, we can be assured He will, on the basis of His promises, answer our prayer. We can pray with confidence.

His changelessness is also an encouragement for our witness and service. Because God does not change His method of making us children of God, we can witness with complete confidence. I know without a doubt when I tell a person that he can become God's child by accepting the work of Jesus Christ on the cross, he will become a child of God. What an encouragement for witness!

On the other hand, the immutability of God is bad news for the sinner. You see, God does not change His attitude toward sin. His knowledge remains always the same. He knows every individual. His attitude toward sin is such that no sinner can hope to be reconciled to God apart from believing in the Lord Jesus Christ. We need to recognize that and we need to make it known to those outside of Christ. God will judge sinners, but God has also said He will forgive sin if the sinner will by faith come and confess the Lord Jesus Christ and accept Him as his personal Saviour.

Because God does not change, we know He will indeed perform what He has said. Our God is an immutable God and we can build our lives upon this.

2. His Wisdom

Some theologians combine the wisdom of God with the knowledge of God, but I would like to view each as a separate characteristic.

What is wisdom? The Greeks called a man wise if he proved his knowledge of a craft or art. If he could make a beautiful sculpture, for instance, he was called a wise man. Later, the Greeks applied the term to an individual who contemplated philosophy, or one who understood life. They used this as a basis for other inquiry.

Our use of the word wisdom has neither of these two meanings. To us, wisdom means the ability to judge correctly and, on the basis of that judgment, to follow the soundest course of action. Wisdom is usually considered to be based on knowledge, experience and understanding.

Our problem, of course, is that we do not always know whether we are working toward the right end. But God, being God, knows exactly what should be achieved. He knows what is the correct end; He can always choose flawlessly. He alone can be truly wise in this way.

Once again, the other attributes of God come into play. God alone is omniscient or all-knowing. He is the only being who fully knows all circumstances. It follows then, according to that definition, that God alone has true wisdom. We may know the circumstances immediately surrounding us, but we do not know *all* the circumstances, and therefore, we cannot always demonstrate wisdom.

Wisdom is also demonstrated by acting according to correct reason and judgment. Sin, however, has affected our wisdom. Our reasoning power is often faulty as is our ability to judge.

Have you ever wondered why someone who has the same basic information as you can arrive at a different conclusion? You say to yourself, "How can he be so blind? Doesn't he understand I'm right, that this is what we ought to do?" The other person probably is saying the same thing about you.

The problem is that we do not always reason correctly. We do not always come to the right judgment. God, because He is a perfect being, always understands. He makes the correct judgment and, thus, His wisdom is true wisdom. It is unlimited. It is faultless.

One basic difference between wisdom and knowledge is that wisdom is practical. Knowledge is knowing and understanding something. We may understand on the basis of the knowledge gained from previous experience. Wisdom deals with actually making decisions and carrying out those decisions. Wisdom is drawing correct conclusions based upon our knowledge. We may *know,* for example, that when it snows in the morning it takes a little longer to get to work. If we are *wise,* we will leave home a few minutes sooner.

Let me illustrate. It snowed one night not long ago

and was still snowing when I got up the next morning. When I saw the ground covered with snow, I asked my wife, "Honey, will you have breakfast ready a few minutes early so I can leave before the traffic gets heavy?"

I got to my office without a problem. Because there were few cars on the streets, I missed only one stoplight the whole way, and thus did not have to stop on inclines.

A short while later another faculty member stopped in my office. "Man," he said, "was it rough getting to school this morning! All those people on the road who don't know how to drive in the snow!" On the basis of his knowledge of the driving conditions he should have been wise enough to leave early.

Unlike our knowledge, God's knowledge is perfect. He understands all things. His wisdom is perfect because He does understand all things. He resolves all things correctly. All His decisions to act are right because He is perfect in all His being. Again, wisdom is the power or ability to judge rightly and then follow the soundest course of action. Wisdom in our case is based upon knowledge. Experience enters in as well. In God's case, experience is not a prerequisite for either His understanding or His knowledge. He knows because He is God. On the other hand, God, because of His infinite understanding, is also all-wise.

Remember, keep all the other attributes of God in mind as well. His wisdom does not grow; it does not diminish. It does not change because His is immutable. His justice and holiness will always cause Him to do what is right.

God cannot gain in wisdom. A man may grow wiser because his knowledge increases. Furthermore, as he increases his knowledge and experience, man can make better judgments and better determine a course of action. In the case of God, however, this is not true. His wisdom is simply a part of His essence or being. It does not change.

God alone is truly wise. He knows all things. Isaiah asks some poignant questions. He asks who counseled God and who instructed Him (Isaiah 40).

The answer is no one. God does not need counsel because He is all-wise. If we are wise, we will ask someone else for advice when we are faced with a problem. However, God does not do that. God is the One who understands all things. His wisdom is perfect. It is never wrong.

What about proof for God's wisdom? Daniel 2:20 says wisdom belongs to God. Without wisdom God could not govern the world. God is in control of the world regardless of what we may think. Men may think they dominate the world, but they don't. Satan thinks he is in control, but he isn't either. God is in control. Without wisdom, it would be impossible for God to govern and control the world.

Men give evidence of wisdom, but that very fact must mean God also has wisdom because He created mankind.

Man is patterned after God, at least as far as his original nature is concerned. Man, to some extent, is wise because God is wise. Although man's wisdom is limited, the very fact that he exhibits wisdom indicates that God must also be wise.

Above and beyond all of these arguments, though, is the Scripture which says that God is the source of all wisdom. Daniel 2:20, 21 and Job 32:8 make it clear that God is indeed the God of wisdom. Keep in mind the distinction between wisdom and knowledge. Knowledge is understanding. For man, this is the basis of wisdom. Wisdom, on the other hand, looks at the ability or power to choose the best course of action and then carry out that action. God has both and so He is all-wise.

I suppose if you are like I am, there are times when you wish you had more wisdom. There are times when I must make a decision for which I do not have the proper background of information or knowledge to determine the proper course of action. Neither do I have the experience that might help. It is then that I wish I had more wisdom.

How is God's wisdom shown to man? Can we see that God is truly wise? First of all, the creation of God demonstrates the wisdom of God. Romans 1:20 says the things of the invisible God may be known through the visible things of God, that is, His creation. We can learn some things about the invisible God by studying creation. For example, we see the wisdom of God in the order manifested in creation.

Dr. John Brumbaugh, Professor of Cell Biology and Genetics at the University of Nebraska—Lincoln, says, "The complexity of living material, its fine detail and its extreme mathematical order at the level of individual molecules point toward God. I have had the privilege of observing some aspects of this in great detail. They are very convincing!''

God's ability to govern and control all things gives us an understanding of Him. Proverbs 3:19 says that by wisdom God created the earth. On the basis of understanding, knowledge and ability, God determined He would create and so He did. Psalm 104:24 says, ''[From] wisdom hast thou made them all.'' From the context, it is clear this verse refers to creation. We know God created a beautiful universe. It is well known that no two snowflakes are alike. Each is individually made. When magnified, each snowflake becomes an awe-inspiring work of art.

Growing up on a Nebraska farm, I used to stand and look at the frost pictures on the windows. The frosted glass God made was incomparably more exquisite than the frosted picture window in the door my parents had purchased at the lumber yard.

God's creative work is manifestation of His wisdom as well as of His glory and omnipotence. We know the order of creation demonstrates the wisdom of God. We also see how creation is moving toward its intended end.

Science is able to predict the orbit of the various planets and other stellar bodies because of the precision with which God created them. Because God in His wisdom made the universe as He did, scientists can shoot satellites from the earth which, years later, fly by Mars, Venus and Saturn, sending back pictures which give information about those planets. God's power keeps the planets from wobbling in their orbit but His wisdom is the basis for the plan, its being carried out and its final ending.

We also see the wisdom of God manifested in the government of men. His government is seen particularly in the laws He gives to men. Man may not acknowledge it, but the law God gives fits man. It is just what man needs. If man accepts this and acts upon that law, he will discover it is right for him. Following the law of God leads to happiness, true happiness. It is not the kind of happiness for which the world is looking. That happiness is so ephemeral it disappears almost with the blink of the eye. A person can be exuberant one moment and the next moment be so down the change is almost unbelievable.

The things of the world cannot give true happiness because they do not last. But when we accept the laws of God and act upon them, we discover those laws do lead to true happiness. Not only do they lead to true happiness, but they benefit man. God knows us better than we can know ourselves and therefore He sets up a proper law to govern us. If we would only follow that law, we would discover we truly benefit by it.

We are told in Romans 2:14 that Gentiles do the law by nature. The Apostle Paul, inspired by the Spirit of God, pointed out to the Jewish leaders they were going to be judged by the law. But the Gentiles are going to be judged without law because they have a law they follow by nature. This, again, indicates the wisdom of God.

The fact that God rewards men for studying His law proves God's wisdom. Psalm 19 says God rewards men for studying His laws. This indicates wisdom because many of us would not bother to study His law unless we received some reward. God understands and, on the basis of His understanding, He establishes the best way to motivate men to study.

It is rather interesting that one of the current concepts of teaching and motivating people to learn involves almost instantaneous reward. If the teacher wants a student to learn something and remember it, she rewards the student as soon as the student gives the correct answer. God used this concept when He gave the law and asked us to study it. If we study it, He will reward us.

We also see God's wisdom in the Word of God as a whole. You see, the revelation of God was given to meet man's need. It was not given all at once, but God in His wisdom gave the revelation that was needed at a given point in the history of men. His revelation was always adequate, sufficient for the need at that given moment.

His wisdom is also seen in His control of sin. The Scriptures are clear that God brings glory to Himself out of the way in which He deals with sin. The Old Testament is full of illustrations of God using sinful instruments to carry out His own means. God used sinful men when they did not realize they were being used. God still uses sinful men to accomplish His own end. To take someone who is violently opposed to Him and use that person to bring about God's own plan and purpose in time clearly illustrates the wisdom of God.

The holocaust of World War II is an example of this. The Nazis destroyed millions of Jews but God used that event to make His people once again recognize they are unique. Although Jewish families had lived in other countries for generations, they were not really assimilated into the population. That holocaust not only reminded the Jews of their special position, but it brought about the nation of Israel. God in His wisdom provided a homeland for His people. He turned the evil of men to His own purpose and brought some good out of it.

The fact that He brings good out of sin also shows His wisdom. This particularly concerns the child of God. Have you discovered that sometimes the end result of a sin you have committed really turns out to be for your good because of what God does for you and to you through that sin? Now, I do not advocate that you sin for that reason, but if you find yourself caught in sin and you take care of it, you may discover God brought something good out of it. This, I believe, is a clear illustration or proof of God's wisdom.

God's plan of redemption clearly demonstrates His wisdom. Scripture teaches the Lord Jesus Christ was born at the precise moment to deal with the problem of sin. Galatians says He was born in "the fullness of the time." God's timing was perfect (Galatians 4:4).

When Christ was born, there was basically one government, that of Rome. Within the confines of the empire there was peace. Because of the complex network of Roman roads, travel was possible so the message of the gospel could spread quickly. Furthermore, although the legal language of the Roman Empire was Latin, Greek was the common language in the Eastern Mediterranean. This also made possible the rapid spread of the gospel. In addition, there was one legal system in force throughout the empire which again helped the spread of the gospel.

What should this mean to us? The fact that we have a God who is all-wise should cause us to trust Him. If He knows all things, and has all wisdom so He makes proper decisions based upon His knowledge, I can trust Him. I can trust His will for my life. I know what He determines for me will be best for me. Romans 12:1-2 is true.

Furthermore, I should appeal to Him for wisdom. The Apostle James says, "If any of you lack wisdom, let him ask of God" (James 1:5). Here the wisdom which we are to request is help to understand temptation. We need to appeal to God for wisdom and He will give it to us. Since God's wisdom is the basis for His judgment, we ought to trust even those judgments which involve us. He knows all about us. He knows all about our circumstances. He knows all that is going to happen to us in the future. Therefore, His judgment is proper and right. It is a wise judgment and we should trust Him.

It should comfort us to know God is all-wise, that He will make proper decisions and carry them out. This should cause us to rely on the judgment of our God in times of difficulty and, thus, be comforted.

We ought also to submit to His wisdom. Why

should I pit my feeble wisdom against the wisdom of the Almighty God? I would be foolish. Yet, so often I am guilty of this. The fact that God is all-wise should cause us to submit willingly to Him.

Finally, we ought to worship this kind of God. We ought to pour out our hearts before Him in praise, adoration and thanksgiving, because our God will do what is best for each of us. His will is good and perfect and acceptable.

3. His Omniscience

The omniscience of God means that He has infinite knowledge and understanding, that He knows everything. Many passages of Scripture prove this. Let me simply refer to one verse as we begin our study. "Great is our Lord, and of great power: his understanding is infinite" (Psalm 147:5).

I am sure many people would like to have more knowledge or understanding. It is difficult for us to understand that God does not need more knowledge but that He has all-knowledge.

Although theologians discuss the omniscience of God with the wisdom of God, it is possible to separate them. At least, some theologians do. In this study, we have looked at the wisdom and now we want to think about His omniscience or knowledge.

What is knowledge? For us, there are several kinds of knowledge. There are some things we know now. That is present knowledge. However, we also have knowledge from past events or experiences. This is remembering or remembrance. That is past knowledge. Knowing the future is foreknowledge. It is knowledge of something that is yet to happen.

Although man makes these distinctions in time, there is no such distinction with God. He is outside of time. Time has no real bearing on Him. Distinctions of time cannot limit His understanding as it does ours. God must be all-knowing. If we are to have full knowledge of the past, present and the future, we must have that same quality or ability, and of course we do not.

Knowledge can be not only past, present and future, from our point of view, but it can also be inherent or intuitive. For instance, we talk about a woman's intuition.

"Honey," my wife, Ruth, said when I came home from work one day, "I think we ought to pick the last of our tomatoes tonight."

Rather surprised, I looked at her. "Why do you say that? The sun is shining brightly. We should have nice weather for a long time yet."

"I don't know. I just think we ought to," she told me.

"Did you hear the weather forecast?"

"No, I just feel like we're going to have frost."

"Well, I don't know," I told Ruth as we started for the garden after the evening meal. "This is awfully early for frost."

I worked my way among the plants and picked the plump red tomatoes. One by one I tossed them to her as she put them in a basket.

To the weatherman's and my surprise, a cold front moved in from the West that night. A killing frost touched the plants. Had we not picked the tomatoes, they would have been frozen.

"I don't know how you did it, but you were right," I conceded.

Whether we like it or not, there does seem to be something to that kind of knowledge. As far as God is concerned it is more than that. God knows just because He knows. It is not something that He has learned. No one has instructed Him. God knows. He has inherent knowledge.

On the other hand, the knowledge of God is not limited to inherent knowledge, but there is a practical aspect to His knowledge. God knows all that goes on. He knows all the experiences that we have. He has practical or experiential knowledge as well as inherent or intuitive knowledge. God knows all things.

Furthermore, we need to understand that His knowledge is infinite. He understands *all* things. There is no limit upon His knowledge. His knowledge cannot increase. No one teaches Him. No one instructs Him. He simply *knows.* Because He is immutable, there is no change in His knowledge. Because He is all-present, He knows everything that goes on throughout the universe. He knows what happens to us as individuals. God is all-knowing from the standpoint of inherent knowledge as well as from the standpoint of practical or experiential knowledge.

What does God know or what is included in His knowledge? The answers to this question may help clarify the definition of God's knowledge. God knows Himself perfectly. This is something that human beings attempt to do. Psychologists tell us that when we come to a full understanding of ourselves, we are truly wise. After finding yourself in a circumstance, have you ever asked yourself, "Now why in the world did I do that?"

We cannot understand certain aspects of our being. God, on the other hand, fully understands Himself. No one else can say that of himself.

God not only knows Himself perfectly, but God knows all things. He knows all things that are possible and all things that are impossible.

It is true that He may, of His own will, limit His knowledge. One of my daughters asked me one day, "If God is all-knowing and all-powerful, how can He say, 'Your sins and iniquities will I remember no more'?"

I explained to her that this does not mean He is incapable of remembering. Rather, God has exercised His own will in this respect and He chooses not to remember. It does not mean that He cannot remember, but simply that He will not. It does not limit His omniscience.

God fully knows His own power, and He alone knows His own full power. Some years ago a gasoline truck crashed on a busy highway. The cab door jammed so tightly rescuers were unable to free the driver. Just as another motorist approached the scene, the truck burst into flames.

The motorist brought his automobile to a halt then dashed to the flaming vehicle. With one great burst of energy he wrenched open the door and pulled out the driver just before flames engulfed the cab. It was discovered later that the man had lost his wife and family in a fire, and the memory of that scene had enabled him to exert superhuman strength.

Scientists believe man uses only about two percent of his brain power. That is rather poor. Yet, God fully knows His own ability and can use it. God knows exactly what He is capable of doing.

God knows all past events, present things and things that can happen in the future. He also knows His creatures. He knows us more fully than we know ourselves. God knows our actions and our thoughts. He knows whether they are good or bad. God understands what we think. This is why the Lord Jesus Christ says that it is as sinful to think the thoughts as it is to do the actions. We must admit that sin does begin in the mind.

How is God's knowledge proven or demonstrated? Scripture clearly sets forth the fact that God is all-knowing. Prophecy proves this knowledge. Are you aware that many, many prophecies were given hundreds of years before their fulfillment? As Scripture explains it, anyone who prophesied had to receive the ability from God Himself. Without God's enablement, human beings could not have prophesied as it occurs in Scripture.

According to Scriptural standards, a true prophet had to meet rigid requirements to prove the validity of his prophecy. To illustrate, the prophecy could not happen by sheer chance. It had to be something that could happen only because the individual knew this was God's plan.

In connection with Christ's birth, death and resurrection alone, hundreds of prophecies have been fulfilled in most minute detail. The only way these prophecies could have been foretold was for God to have exercised His knowledge. He alone has knowledge of the future. He imparted this knowledge to His prophets so they could give the information to the people when He wanted it given. Prophecy is indeed proof of the knowledge of God.

God's dealings with man also demonstrate that God is all-knowing. God knows the thoughts and intent of the person's heart. He does not have to be told; He just knows. When Christ was on earth, He often answered the unspoken questions of the crowd. Often someone asked Him a question but the question verbalized was not the question in the mind of the inquirer. To the astonishment of the speaker, Christ answered the unspoken question, the question still in the speaker's mind. This clearly proves He knew the thoughts and intent of the individual. We see God's omniscience or knowledge in His ability to know what men are thinking and in His ability to respond.

Our knowledge comes from study or experience. We are not born with much knowledge, at least as far as we can tell. God however knows, not by seeing the things in His own mind, but by seeing Himself. Once again, God fully knows Himself. He is responsible for all that exists, whether in time or eternity because there is no difference to Him. He knows the potential for everything. God knows simply by seeing Himself. However, it is not that He sees the thing in His mind as we do. We can gain knowledge of something by sitting down and thinking for a while. We see certain things in our mind. We may think our way through a series of arguments. We study the pros and cons on which we finally base our decision. Having considered the possibilities, we know what to do. We see in our minds. We see the action; see the potentialities. God merely sees Himself. He understands Himself because He is the essential cause of all that exists. He simply wills and things are.

Since our understanding is limited, it is difficult for us to understand this. Nevertheless, as far as we can understand how God knows, this is the way He knows: He knows because He fully understands Himself. Scripture says when we stand before our Lord Jesus Christ we shall know even as we are known. This means that one day our knowledge of ourselves will be perfect or complete, just as God's knowledge of us is complete and perfect. It would seem, then, that we too will have the ability to know simply because we understand ourselves fully.

We arrive at our knowledge by a process of reasoning. By thinking through a series of logical steps, we arrive at a valid conclusion. God, however, does not know by reason; He knows by what we may speak of as intuition. He knows inherently because of Who and What He is. God is omnipresent so He sees all that is occurring. He does not gain knowledge by His individual senses. He sees all things and understands.

We, of course, not only gain knowledge by reasoning, but we receive much of our knowledge by way of our physical senses. This is especially true of the young child. We really don't know if the young child can reason. Until the child can express himself with language, it is difficult to tell whether or not he actually is capable of reasoning. We do know, however, that the child learns many things by the physical senses. He learns very quickly when something is hot or cold. He learns when something is bitter or sweet. It does not take a great deal of experience. A child learns by his senses, but God does not. He does not taste something and say, "Hm, this is sweet;" or "Oh, this is sour. I don't think I'll eat this anymore." God simply knows. He knows by virtue of who and what He is.

We not only learn by reasoning and by our physical senses; we also learn by receiving instruction. I hope that you are learning something and that you are increasing your knowledge of the nature of God through these studies. On the other hand, God does not receive instruction; He knows. We can listen to someone else and learn something we did not know before. We say, "I didn't know that." God does not learn that way. He simply knows.

Sometimes we gain more knowledge on the basis of what we already know. However, nothing that God knows is the cause of His knowledge. Because we know something is true, we arrive at the understanding of something else. We say, because something is true, it then follows that something else must also be true. In contrast, nothing God knows is the cause of additional knowledge on His part because He knows all things.

God also knows all things distinctly and completely. Our knowledge often is not distinct. It is a mass of knowledge. We do not completely understand

41

everything, but God does know all things distinctly and completely.

Since God is immutable, it logically follows that His knowledge cannot change or vary. God knows; He does not gain knowledge; He does not lose knowledge. It is hard for us to understand this because we change in our knowledge. We forget and we gain knowledge. But not God. God is all-knowing. There is no variation in His knowledge.

What should this mean to us? If God knows us, and He does, we must seek God if we want to know ourselves. When we come to know God, we come to know and understand ourselves.

It also follows that if God knows all things, He must be in control of all things. Unless this were true, something which He did not know could occur. If there were some lack in His knowledge, when the unknown occurred, God would gain knowledge. This cannot be true. Nothing can occur of which God is unaware.

Since God is all-knowing, it logically follows that someday there will be a day of judgment. That judgment day will be a proper day of judgment. He will judge individuals according to their merit. That is, He will judge the sinner on the basis of the light that he had.

He will also judge those of us who are born again, but it will not be judgment for our merit. It will be judgment based on the merit of the Lord Jesus Christ. There will, however, be judgment. It will be a right judgment because God is all-knowing. There is no possibility of the judgment miscarrying because of unknown facts. In our earthly court system, justice may miscarry because no one knows all the facts in a particular situation, but not so with God.

The very fact that God is all-knowing should cause us to believe and trust in the promises of God. After all, God knows what is going to happen. He knows our situation. If God promises something, He can fulfill that promise.

On the other hand, I can promise something and it does not always work out. I tried to keep my promises to my children, but sometimes I had to break them.

Quite frequently, when I was a pastor, we had to change family plans. One year we took a camping trip to the Black Hills. We had set up our tent and equipment with plans to spend a week. Early in the week, however, a message reached us with the sad news that one of our church members had died unexpectedly and the family needed their pastor. We struck the tent and started for home.

"I'm sorry, kids," I told the family, "but we'll have to break our promise."

The children understood but they were also disappointed. God never disappoints us by failing to fulfill a promise. He knows all things.

An awareness of His omniscience should cause us to avoid judging others. God is all-knowing and He knows us fully. He knows us even more completely than we know ourselves. God is the One, and the only One, who can adequately judge.

His omniscience should also comfort us. You may have a real desire to walk with God, a real desire to please Him. Deep down in your heart this is what you want to do. Nevertheless, in your daily experiences you may fall short of what you would like to be. God knows. To me, it is comforting to know that God knows my real desire to walk with Him and to please Him. He knows my desire to do His will and when I fail, that knowledge comforts me.

His omniscience should also lead us to bow down in worship and adoration. It should cause us to please God and become more like Him.

One other thing ought to be apparent. Since God is all-knowing, as He is, the sinner should stop to consider his way. We cannot hide from God. We cannot somehow pull the wool over His eyes. We cannot assume that He does not understand what we are doing. God knows. God knows our thoughts. God knows exactly what we are and what we are doing. Therefore, the sinner ought to recognize this and act upon it. The only solution to the sinner's problem is to believe in Jesus Christ. Our God is an all-knowing God.

4. His Dominion or Sovereignty

"The Lord hath prepared his throne in the heavens; and his kingdom ruleth over all" (Psalm 103:19). What is God's dominion? It is God's ability or right to do what He wills. Since God is sovereign, or has all dominion, He can do what He wills to do. It is lawful and right. The omnipotence looks at God's physical power, or His *ability* to do what He wants to do. His sovereignty, on the other hand, means He has the *right,* that it is morally correct for Him to do as He wishes. The two attributes are closely related. Yet, they are different.

Here again, when we discuss His sovereignty we must keep all the other attributes in mind. For instance, because God is good, He never uses His sovereignty in an unworthy way. He never does anything that is evil toward His creatures. He does only that which is good. He cannot do otherwise for He is a good God. God never uses His dominion or sovereignty in any way that would contradict His other attributes. Because God is holy, He will do nothing that is sinful. Because He is just, He will do nothing that is unfair. Because He is immutable, His dominion can never increase or decrease. All His other attributes affect His sovereignty.

His dominion is based upon the excellency of His nature. Since God is God, He is perfect. He has all the attributes that make Him the kind of being that He is. God's dominion is simply based upon the excellency of His nature because of who and what He is. He has dominion or sovereignty over all things.

God's acts of creation give Him the authority to have all dominion. He can do what He desires with His own creation for He is responsible for all that exists. It is morally correct for Him to do as He desires with it.

Scripture illustrates this by referring to the potter and the clay. It teaches that the potter has the right to put the clay on the wheel. He can make whatever he wants out of that piece of clay. Once he has made it, he has the right to dispose of it as he sees fit. If he chooses to break the piece of pottery and throw it away, it is his right. The potter can make the pottery into something honorable that would be fit for a palace, or he can, for example, design it to be a slop jar. You see, it is the potter who determines what the clay will become and how it will be used.

If this is true on this level, then how much more is it true of God with respect to the universe. God as the Creator can do as He desires with His creation and it is morally right for Him to do so.

God also has dominion over all things because of the benefits He bestows on all things. Salvation is an example of this. Certainly those of us who have accepted by faith the work of Christ on the cross should acknowledge the sovereignty of God in our lives. He has not only created us, but He has also bought us with a price. He has redeemed us. He purchased us out of the marketplace and now we belong to Him, not only by right of creation but also by right of purchase. This certainly should prove to us that God has dominion over us.

However, even as God's children, we do not like to admit He has authority over us. We do not like to admit that He is in control. This attitude, of course, gets us into trouble. Our refusal to recognize His dominion over our lives results in catastrophe. Although we do not like to acknowledge His sovereignty, Scripture leaves no doubt that He is Lord over all.

What is the nature of God's dominion? God's authority is independent. He does not receive it from any source. He has it simply because He is God. Again, it is based on the excellency of His nature, His creative act and His preservation of this creation. No one has given God His dominion or sovereignty. It is independent of all other things. If His dominion depended upon someone's giving it to Him, God, of course, would not truly be God. He would be subservient to the person who gave Him dominion. But God is indeed over all. His dominion is just a part of what He is.

God's dominion is absolute. He is free to do anything He desires to do. There is no one or nothing that compels Him to do anything. His dominion is free from all law. There is no standard to which He is circumscribed. God answers to no one because He is God. Most of us, even if we have some authority, usually are answerable to someone. There are few people in the world who do not ultimately have to answer to some other human being. God, however, answers to no one. His dominion is absolute.

The dominion of God is irresistible. When God commands, it is done. When I went into the military service, the men in command did their best to give us a good introduction to our new life. One officer put it rather eloquently. "O.K." he said. "When I command you to jump, jump, and on the way up, ask, 'How high, sir?' "

That is somewhat like God. When He says that something is to be done, it is done. God, however, does not exercise His dominion as a tyrant. He does not force His dominion upon anyone. He wants us to freely recognize it. Whether or not we realize it, God is in control, but He is never malicious nor evil in His use of this attribute.

It is important to realize that His dominion is over all. Some individuals do not believe in God. This does not make any difference; God still continues to exist. There are those who do not believe God has all dominion; but He does.

His dominion is eternal. The fact that He created the world and the universe does not mean that He did not have dominion prior to that time. It is true that when He created the world and the universe, they then came under His authority. However, He had all authority before that. His dominion is eternal. It is a part of what He is. He always has had dominion and He always will.

How does God show His dominion? First of all, He shows it by His laws. We call them natural laws, but there really are no natural laws. They are God's laws. God says that the seasons will continue. Spring follows winter and summer follows spring; autumn follows summer and then we have winter again. God says these seasons will continue until He finally wraps up all things. These are laws only because God has established them.

The earth continues to rotate on its axis and revolve around the sun in its pattern because God says that is what it is going to do. He also has established the law of planting and harvest. After the farmer plants, he reaps the harvest. This operates in the realm of the spiritual as well. If a person sows corruption, he will reap corruption. If he sows evil, he will reap evil. If he sows good; he will reap good. A farmer who sows wheat will get wheat. If he sows corn, he will get corn. That is one of the laws which God has established. He shows His dominion by these laws which He has established.

God not only shows His dominion by setting up laws, but He also shows it by setting aside laws. Contrary to what some people believe, God did stop the earth's spinning on its axis for a period of time. The Book of Joshua tells us about this.

To some extent, science and its findings would tend to support this. The tilt of the earth, the angle of the axis of the earth in relation to the sun has changed. The North Pole area has shifted. It is possible that some of this occurred during the long day in the Book of Joshua. If the earth shifted properly, it would cause it to change in relationship to its rotation around the sun. This would cause a long day. God can set aside His laws.

We see another illustration of this when Jesus stilled the water in the Sea of Galilee. You remember Jesus was sleeping in the bottom of the boat when the storm arose. The frightened disciples awakened Him. "Don't you care that we perish?"

Jesus arose and calmly said, "Peace, be still."

Immediately the wind stopped blowing and the waves stopped crashing against the sides of the boat. You see, Jesus, being God, had dominion over all things. The men in the boat recognized this and exclaimed, "What manner of man is this because even the winds and the waves obey Him?"

Xerxes, the king who attempted to conquer Greece, had the Hellespont punished with forty lashes when the waves destroyed his bridge. Nevertheless, it did not stop the waves. Winds and waves do not normally obey men, but they obeyed Jesus Christ because He was more than man. He was God.

God's dominion is also shown in His ability to judge and punish those who do not follow the standards of conduct which He establishes. This standard is the righteous standard of God as seen in Scripture. God judges those who break these laws. We have many examples of this in Scripture, particularly in the Old Testament. While individuals think they can get by and break the law of God, judgment will come.

God also reveals His sovereignty by calling those whom He pleases and by bestowing grace upon them. The Scripture clearly states that we come unto God because He calls us, and He calls whom He pleases. We cannot command God to save a person. All we can do is present the claims of Christ to the individual. We can explain the way of salvation to him and then, if God calls, the person responds.

We also see God's dominion by His governing of the world. God does control the world. From the Scriptures it is clear God moves men and nations in accordance with His will. God used the Babylonians under Nebuchadnezzar to bring judgment upon the southern kingdom of Israel. God also brought judgment upon King Nebuchadnezzar for failure to recognize God as God. Ultimately, of course, the nation of Babylon itself was destroyed. Again, this was because God was in control. He exercises dominion and governs the world.

God also demonstrates His dominion in His plan of redemption. God Himself is the Redeemer. God Himself is the One who planned the way of salvation. This shows His dominion.

If God has all control over everything, what does it mean to us? It should, once again, be a comfort to us. In looking at the world around us, some say, "Well, if we've got a God who is in control of all things, He must be a terrible God. I ought to be afraid of Him."

On the contrary His dominion ought to comfort us. God, being God, having dominion over all things, can pardon whom He wills. Then, if I by faith come and accept Jesus Christ, God says my sins are forgiven. When He declares me justified on the basis of the blood of His Son, I have been justified. God has dominion and He can do what He wants to do because of His omnipotence. It is morally right for Him to do what He wants to do.

Since He has dominion over all things, it means He can provide for us. Recently, when I met for prayer with a group of students, one student expressed praise for answered prayer. He had asked God for money to meet a bill of $400. Just before we met, a check for $200 had arrived in the mail.

"God can provide," he told us.

Why can God provide? Because He is in dominion. He can move individuals and cause them to do what is necessary to meet other people's needs. God can provide because He controls all things.

God can protect us, as well. We see this in the case of Job. When Satan wanted to test Job, God said, "All right, you go ahead, but you can't touch Job's life."

God protected Job and Satan could only do that which God allowed. Now, I don't know about you, but that's a comforting thought. Satan is far superior to me but in God He cannot touch me unless God allows it.

Because He has dominion, we should trust Him. Since He will exercise His dominion only in a way that will not violate His basic personality or violate His other attributes, we can trust Him. We can be assured that He will do what is best for us. We know that He will do whatever He says He will.

God's sovereignty should also cause us to worship Him. How amazing to have this kind of God! He alone is worthy of all worship. He does only what is always morally right. Certainly, He is worthy of our praise.

On the other hand, God's sovereignty ought to do something for the sinner, as well. Since God has dominion over all, He can do what He wants to the sinner. He will not be arbitrary with the sinner; He will not do anything that is unjust. But He will give the sinner exactly what is right. According to God's Word, the sinner who rejects the free gift of salvation will be separated from God forever. He will be eternally damned. Punishment is inescapable. There is no way out. Even death will not hide the sinner from judgment, for Scripture declares that one day everyone will stand in God's presence. The unjust, those who have not trusted Christ for salvation, will be cast into the lake of fire. For the unsaved person, the dominion of God should be a frightening thing. Recognizing that judgment is coming, the sinner should lose no time in coming to the Saviour. God has all dominion and He will punish sin.

5. His Omnipotence

Our God is an all-powerful God. He is omnipotent, having unlimited power or authority. Because our power is limited, it is difficult to comprehend what it means to have complete power. It is true that some people have more power than others, but man's power is limited in one way or another. God alone has all-power.

Some use the word "authority" to define the power of God. This means that He has the right to control individuals. God has that authority. He is in a position of superiority over others, but it is more than that. God not only has the power to act, but He has the strength. This is something we as men and women really do not have. We may have certain power, but we do not have the strength to do everything that we will to do.

God never uses all of His power. None of His actions have ever required Him to exert the fullness of His power. This is hard for us to understand.

Where we live, we can expect snow in the wintertime. Sometimes the snow piles deep enough and the streets get icy enough for our cars to get stuck. One winter, a few years ago, I got stuck as I was coming up the hill to our home. I walked to the house and asked my wife to get behind the wheel so I could push the car out of the snow. I pushed and I pushed and I pushed some more. All of a sudden, the car moved and we were out of the snow. I stood there. My legs quivered. I could not move. Why? Because I had exerted my strength to such an extent that my muscles had become filled with weights that had not yet been carried away by the blood. There just was no more strength there. I had used all of it for the moment. God never finds Himself in that situation. He never has exerted all His power.

God's power is what enables Him to bring about that which His wisdom and holiness lead Him to do. God in His wisdom, His understanding and His knowledge knows exactly what He ought to do. His omnipotence, or His power, enables Him to *do* that. His wisdom and holiness give Him the basis on which He acts. His omnipotence is the power to act.

The omnipotence of God is also the basis for using His other attributes. God can do whatever He desires. God is able to be everywhere. God is all-knowing. These things are true because He has all power.

God's power is infinite and it is immutable. We may exhaust our power, but when God uses His power, it never diminishes in any way, nor does He ever do anything which increases His power. When our son was in junior high school, he wanted a set of weights to develop his muscles. Of course, he could have developed them by pushing the lawn mower in the summer and shoveling snow in the winter! Nevertheless, he wanted weights and we got them for him for Christmas. Day after day he used those weights to build his muscles. But God does not develop His power that way. His power is always there.

What God has done does not limit His power. God exhibited His power in His creative activity, but God could produce more and better objects if He wished.

While God has all power, He never uses His power to do anything contrary to what He is. Campers often try to stump me by asking the question, "If God has all power, can He die?" They think they have me.

I tell them, "Yes, God could die, but it is impossible for Him to die because He is truly life. He does not exercise His power to give up His life because He also is life, and He can never die."

God never does anything contrary to His will or what He is. For example, God will not use His power to justify a sinner in any other way but through faith in Jesus Christ. He has the power and the authority to justify in any way He chooses, but He has said men can be justified only by faith in Jesus Christ. Therefore, that is the only way He will save men.

God does not use His power to go contrary to His nature. When He says He will do something one way, He will not use His power to do it some other way, unless that is part of His will. He has the ability to act and to carry out what He desires in accordance with His will.

Scripture tells us the work of creation is an evidence of His power. Isaiah 40 clearly indicates that creation did not cause God too much trouble. In creating, God measured the waters—the oceans—in the hollow of His hand. He measured out the heaven with the span of His hand. Astronomers still are not completely sure how big space really is. They are hoping to make some new multiple telescopes that will enable them to see farther into space, but they really do not know its size.

I can tell you how big it is. It is as big as the span of God's hand. The trouble is we do not know the size of God's hand. As a matter of fact, He does not actually have a physical hand; it is a figure of speech. Nevertheless, God knows how big space is. He made it. Scripture says that He measured the dust of the earth in a measure and the mountains in scales, the hills in a balance. He just held it out there and determined what they weighed. Now that eloquently illustrates the power of God. We often think of creation as the most outstanding thing God has done.

Scripture, however, makes it clear that it took more power to bring about the plan of salvation than it did to create the universe. When God carried out His plan of salvation, the Bible declares, He bared His strong right arm. In creation, He used the hollow of His hand; He measured the dust in balances; he used the span of His hand. However, when it came to salvation, the figure of speech is His strong right arm. The greatest work that God has done, the greatest exhibition of His power is in providing salvation. Any time a sinner comes and by faith accepts the Lord Jesus Christ, we see God's power manifested. In that act of faith, the individual is transformed into a saint, a child of God. He has the privilege and the right to have fellowship with the eternal God.

Throughout Scripture there is an emphasis on the fact that God has all-power (Cf. Psalm 115:3; Numbers 11:23; and Daniel 11:36). We can see the power of God in the government of the world. We may not think that God's power is seen there, but when we study the Old Testament we see that God does move men and people to accomplish His will. He has that power or that ability.

We see God's power clearly displayed in His preservation of the universe. Scripture states that it is actually the Lord Jesus Christ who continues to sustain, govern and control the universe. He has that power. The very fact that the universe continues as it does, following so-called natural laws, is an indication of God's power. Scientists admit they really do not know what holds the universe together. According to their understanding, it should fly apart. The Scripture says the power of God holds all things together. We should thank God that He continues to display His power in preserving the universe.

His power is most adequately seen in the Person He used to redeem sinners. It took God Himself to bring the plan of salvation into existence. It took God Himself, the second Person of the Trinity, to manifest Himself on earth so He could redeem men. Certainly this ought to impress upon us, not only the significance of salvation, but the power of God.

God's power is also manifested in the people He

uses to proclaim the gospel message. The Apostle Paul talks about "the foolishness of preaching." If we had had our choice in proclaiming the message, we might not have chosen preaching, and we probably would not have used ourselves. We would have chosen almost any other method, including the use of supernatural beings.

Classes I have taken at the university have brought out the point that the lecture method is one of the weakest teaching methods. It is adequate for getting across lots of material, but it does not hold the attention of the student nor help him retain the material. Yet God used this method. Through the "foolishness of preaching" men are saved. There really is not a lot of methodology or media that can be used in preaching the gospel, but in response to the preaching, people are brought to a knowledge of Jesus Christ. They are transformed and made new creatures.

Certainly, His power is manifested through the people He uses. He uses mere human beings. There is no reason why God could not have said to the Lord Jesus Christ, "When You come back to heaven, I'll use all the legions of angels. I'll send one angel to each person on the earth; he will preach the gospel to him and give him a chance to believe. The whole thing will be over and done with."

God did not plan it that way. Rather, He uses people. If we are honest with ourselves, we must recognize that we are weak individuals, but in our weakness God reveals His power.

God clearly demonstrates His power in the application of redemption. When a person believes, he becomes a new creature. Old things pass away. All things become new. A newly-saved person cannot explain what has happened to him, but he is changed. He is not the same person. This reveals the power of God. God has transformed him and made him into an entirely different person.

What should a knowledge of God's power do for us? First of all, the very fact that God is all-powerful should be a source of comfort and sustenance in times of trouble. God says that He will meet our needs. It should strengthen and comfort us to know that God has the power to do so. He can do whatever is necessary for us in a given situation—without question. If I were the one giving the help, there might be some question, but not with God. God is all-powerful.

Psalm 121:1-2 says our help comes from God. "I will lift up mine eyes unto the hills, from whence cometh my help. My help cometh from the Lord, which made heaven and earth." The verses that follow this passage indicate that God was comforting His people who were in affliction and distress. We too can have help in times of stress. It should comfort us to know God has all power.

God's power is also a help in times of temptation or testing. Again, God says He will be with us and He will meet our needs in all times of temptation. There are many passages of Scripture which support this. I do not know what this means to you, but for me, it is comforting to know God is there, that He will help me in my testings. I do not have to face temptation alone. It says, for example, in Ephesians 6:10,11: "Finally, my brethren, be strong in the Lord, and in the power of his might. Put on the whole armour of God . . . ." The context is looking at a time of temptation and trial. God is there. He will give help.

Because God is all-powerful, we can be assured that He will fulfill the promises He has made. If I make a promise, I may or I may not fulfill it. But if God promises, He has the power to do what He promises. You see, nothing else can interfere.

As registrar of Grace College of the Bible, I am under authority of the President, the Academic Dean and the other members of the administration. Yesterday I made plans to accomplish some necessary things. Before I had started on my plans, however, the Academic Dean asked me to make a report for him. That meant that all the things I had planned to do, all the things I had promised myself I would do, had to go by the board. I did what the Academic Dean wanted me to do.

God is not that way. He is all-powerful. He can do what He wants to do. When He makes a promise, we can be absolutely certain He will fulfill that promise. When God tells me the day will come when I will be conformed to the image of the Lord Jesus Christ, that I will be exactly like Him, I know beyond doubt this promise will be fulfilled—no question.

God's omnipotence ought also to comfort us because we know, in spite of appearances, the church will not be defeated. In the Book of Matthew, the Lord Jesus Christ told the Apostle Peter, when He gave that tremendous confession of faith, He would build His church and the gates of hell would not prevail against it. The verse does not say evil will be unable to overcome the church. Christ says the very gates of hell cannot stand against the church. The members of the church are the ones attacking, on the offense so to speak, and God's power enables them to enter into the very gates of hell and free those people held in bondage of sin.

As we proclaim the gospel and people respond to the gospel, they are set free. We know, even though appearances today would seem to indicate the church is being defeated, this is not the case. God has promised the church will be victorious and we should believe Him. It ought to comfort us to know the church cannot be defeated. God has promised and, because of His omnipotence, He fulfills His promises.

The truth that God is omnipotent should motivate us to witness to the lost. Just as all His promises for the believer will be fulfilled, so will those with respect to the lost. There is no possible way for sinners to escape the judgment of their sins by God. No one has the authority or power to change God's requirements for obtaining eternal life. He has stipulated the sinner may be saved through faith in the Person and work of Jesus Christ. How can the sinner be saved if we do not bring him the gospel? God has all authority; we must obey.

6. His Goodness

What is good? It is hard for us to comprehend someone who is truly good, someone who does not change. We are more familiar with that person in the nursery rhyme who "when she was good, was very, very good, but when she was bad, she was horrid." That's the way we are. We can be good occasionally, but we can also change very quickly and become terrible. Actually, sometimes we think it is unpleasant to be around someone who is good. That person sets our teeth on edge. This cannot be the case with God.

The goodness of God is not the same as His blessedness, nor His holiness, nor His mercy, nor His love, nor His grace. Some theologians group these all together, but I do not believe those elements are necessarily a part of the goodness of God.

The goodness of God is the bounty of our God. It is what leads God to be loving, merciful and kind to men. It is His inclination to deal well with His creatures. The goodness of God is simply the bounty of God.

There is nothing that really forces God to deal well with us. God would be well within His rights if He would wipe us from the face of the earth, but He does not. Why not? Because He is a good God.

Furthermore, the goodness of God is toward all men. Some attributes of God are particularly displayed with respect to the child of God alone. However, when it comes to the goodness of God, God is good to all men. He cares for them. He is inclined to deal well with them. This is why the rain falls upon the just and the unjust. God is a good God.

God's goodness involves all His other attributes. None of them can do away or infringe upon God's goodness. We must keep all the characteristics or attributes of God in balance. Today, for example, many emphasize the love of God at the expense of the holiness and the justice of God. While God is indeed a God of love, He is still a holy God, a righteous God and a just God. Therefore, He will judge the sinner and the saint as well. We cannot emphasize one attribute and ignore the others.

We must also recognize that the goodness of God is infinite. Parents become fully aware of the approaching Christmas season when their children begin to act a bit abnormal. The children become extremely good. They even volunteer to do things without prompting from the parents. The parents, at first observation, may think the child is sick until they realize the Christmas season is nearing. Children somehow seem to get a little bit "gooder" around Christmastime because they hope to get some kind of reward.

God is not that way. God's goodness is infinite. He has always been a good God. He did not become good and He will not cease to be good. He always has been good. That God does not change in His goodness is difficult for us to understand. We have difficulty understanding God is infinitely good. We can be better in some situations than others, but often we find our goodness is rather superficial.

The goodness of God is communicable. God cannot give some of His attributes to His creatures, but He can communicate His goodness. He gives it freely to us. When we accept the Lord Jesus Christ by faith, He looks upon us as good. Our experience may not always match up with our position in Christ; nonetheless, God looks upon us as being good. Our problem is to make our position and our experience match. Since God's goodness is communicable, it means that we too can deal well with the creatures of God, our fellow men.

All that God does is good. We may find it difficult to understand this. Some of the ancient writers had a problem with this. For example, in one of his books Voltaire goes to extreme lengths to write satirically about the best of all possible worlds. All kinds of things happen to his main character. Voltaire tries to show that because of what happens in the experiences of men, it is totally impossible for God to be good. Although we may not always understand the goodness of God we must recognize He is a good God. He does good whether or not we recognize it as good.

One of the reasons God created was because He wanted to display His goodness. If He had not created, God would not be able to manifest His goodness outside the realm or framework of the

Trinity. Because of the creation, God can make His goodness known.

Do we have proof that God is indeed a good God? Christ declares God is good. In Mark 10:17,18 a rich young ruler questions Jesus. "Good Master," he asks, "what shall I do that I may inherit eternal life?"

"Why callest thou me good?" Jesus answers. "There is none good but . . . God."

Exodus 34:6 says God is abundant in goodness. Zechariah 9:17 exclaims, "For how great is his goodness." Other passages of Scripture also speak of this. If you wish to study this further, I suggest you check your concordance. You will find numerous passages to support His goodness.

We can also prove God's goodness from His actual creation. The creation account in Genesis, chapter one, states that when God looked at His creation activity the first day, He said, "It is good." He did this on the following days and on the sixth day, Scripture states He looked at everything He had created and said, "It is very good."

From this we know that all that God created was good as it came from His hand. We know from the argument of cause and effect that God must be greater than what He created. Since everything God created is good, God Himself must also be good.

We can also see God is a good God when we look at His laws and judgments. God's laws and judgments are not set up as a means to punish people. Rather, they are set up so man will know what is a right and proper standard of conduct. The judgments that come are not punishment but are incentives to do good. God does judge us. He does this so we will realize we have transgressed His law and are involved in sin. If He did not judge us, chances are we would continue in our way and sin more and more. As a result, God would heap even greater condemnation upon us. The very fact that God judges us is an indication of His goodness.

God also brings judgment upon sinners. He brings calamities upon them so they will realize there is indeed a God to whom they are responsible. Even in the case of sinners, judgment or difficulty is not an indication of the vindictiveness of God nor the vengeance of God. Rather, God uses this act of goodness to make even the sinner realize he faces a holy, righteous God.

Of course, we who truly know God need to recognize that his judgment, particularly for us, is designed for our benefit. Hebrews, chapter twelve, tells us God chastens every child whom He loves. He does this to strengthen us spiritually, making us more like Himself.

God's goodness may include His love, His mercy and His grace, but I believe it is wider, bigger and more complete than those three attributes.

How does God show His goodness? We have already touched on this in proving the goodness of God. God's creative activity demonstrates His goodness. God did not have to create. God, simply because He is a good God, decided to make His goodness known. According to the Bible, the culmination of His creative activity was the creation of man and it is particularly with respect to man that God manifests His goodness. His creation proceeded from His goodness. It was His first act of goodness. Scripture states that He created man and put him over the whole of His creation. Man was to have dominion. He gave man the use of all the things He had created except the fruit of one tree in the garden. Even after man sinned God continued to manifest His goodness by helping him.

God demonstrates His goodness not only in His creative activity, but He reveals His goodness in preserving creation. Have you ever stopped to think where the world and the universe would be if God did not continue to preserve it? Science says the laws of nature are inexorable; they continue to operate. The laws of nature do not merely exist. God established the laws. Nature follows its so-called laws because God has established them and He preserves them.

We know, for example, from the laws of nuclear physics, much of what we call solid material is actually made up of swiftly moving particles and is largely space. That chair on which you are sitting is largely space. How is it held together? It is the goodness of God. He preserves His creation.

We also see His goodness in the laws He has given to man. We sometimes think the giving of the law was something that was not good for man. But it is really a help to him. It lets man know what standard God wants him to meet. It gives him a standard of right and wrong. Some people become mentally ill because they cannot decide what is right and wrong.

God gave a standard. That standard will clearly indicate what is right and wrong. That is an act of the goodness of God.

God also manifests His goodness in salvation. Remember, God was under no obligation to save mankind. When Adam and Eve sinned in the Garden of Eden, God could just as well have wiped them out and started over again. But God was a good God. God provided salvation.

The act of sin in the Garden of Eden did not catch God by surprise. He knew it was going to happen. Because of His goodness, He had already planned that some day, thousands of years later, the second Person of the Godhead would become incarnate. He would make God truly known to man. He would reveal the goodness of God by going to the cross and dying to pay the penalty for sin which man could not pay. God's goodness is a basis for salvation.

God also reveals His goodness by rewarding us. God is under no obligation to reward us as Christians. According to the Scriptures, if we receive any reward at all at the judgment seat of Christ, it will be simply because we have allowed God, the Holy Spirit, to work through us to accomplish His will. Anything we do in our own strength is simply our own works. These will not stand at the judgment seat of Christ.

It is as though, after assigning a paper to one of my classes, I would say, "Now I realize this paper is far beyond your capabilities. I'm going to write the paper. I'll give you each a copy and you in turn will type the title page, put your name on it and turn it back to me. You will get the grade. Because I have done the chapter and it is exactly what I want, I will give each of you an 'A.' ''

I don't do that, but God does. God does the work through us by His Holy Spirit; then because of His goodness, He rewards us for it.

God's goodness is also manifested in providing Scripture for us. Have you ever stopped to think what a loss it would be to us if we did not have the revelation of God? We would have no basis for any knowledge of Him at all.

God's goodness is also shown toward us in His control of our testings and temptations. He does not allow us to face anything we are unable to bear. This demonstrates His goodness in a very practical way.

What should this mean to us? We ought to be careful not to abuse His goodness by complaining. In the Wilderness on their way from Egypt to the Promised Land, the children of Israel murmured and complained until finally God had to judge them. We should learn from them.

If God does bring us into a hard place, we ought to recognize that He is indeed a good God and we can trust Him. If God brings us into a time of testing, we ought not to manifest a lack of faith. If we truly believe God does not allow us "to be tempted above that which we are able," we should wait upon Him by faith. We ought not to be distrustful of Him.

We ought to do the will of God because we know God is a good God, and He will forgive us of our sin. Be careful! Don't abuse the goodness of God. If we abuse the goodness of God, we should not complain if He judges us. If we complain because God judges us for abuse of His goodness, we compound our sin.

The goodness of God is the basis for God's love and concern for us. It, in turn, ought to make us love Him and be concerned about Him. We ought to be careful not to bring disrepute to His name. God deserves to be loved, but we do not merit love. He loves us because He is good.

Because God is a good God we can trust Him. He will never do anything bad for us. Because He is good, we ought to be able to accept His will for our lives. Romans 12:1,2 says, "I beseech you therefore, brethren, by the mercies of God, that ye present your bodies a living sacrifice, holy, acceptable unto God, which is your reasonable service. And be not conformed to this world: but be ye transformed by the renewing of your mind, that ye may prove what is that good, and acceptable, and perfect, will of God."

God, because He is a good God, has a will for us that is the best it can possibly be. We ought to simply allow Him to work out that will in our lives. Because we know God is good, it is only reasonable to give our lives back to Him. It is a rational decision, not an emotional one. However, we do not want to do this. Somehow we are afraid that if we give God complete control He will give us a life of unpleasantness. It is strange that we could accept God's love for us when we were sinners, but we doubt His love for us as His children. As God's children, God wants only the best for us. Certainly we can fully trust Him to give us what is best for us because He is good.

The goodness of God should comfort us. Because God delights in doing good, He answers our prayers. God is under no compulsion to answer our prayers; because He is good, He does hear and answer. His goodness should help us understand the tests and afflictions which come into our experiences. It should cause us to be happy in spite of difficulties. Above all, it should cause us to serve Him. Because He is good, we ought to do all we can to please Him.

We should stop and meditate upon the goodness of our God. If we think about it and realize He is really a good God, it will lead us to worship Him. It will keep us humble, faithful and patient. Above all, it will keep us thankful because we realize all we have is simply an outpouring of the goodness of God.

The fact that we have a good God should motivate us to be good. We should want to be like Him. He has communicated His goodness to us and, with the power of the Holy Spirit residing within us, we can be people who are good. Our God is a good God and we ought to worship, praise and adore Him.

7. His Holiness

"In the year that king Uzziah died I saw also the Lord sitting upon a throne, high and lifted up, and his train filled the temple. Above it stood the seraphims: each one had six wings; with twain he covered his face, and with twain he covered his feet, and with twain he did fly. And one cried unto another, and said, Holy, holy, holy, is the Lord of hosts: the whole earth is full of his glory.

"Then said I, Woe is me! for I am undone: because I am a man of unclean lips, and I dwell in the midst of a people of unclean lips; for mine eyes have seen the King, the Lord of hosts. Then flew one of the seraphims unto me, having a live coal in his hand, which he had taken with the tongs from off the altar: And he laid it upon my mouth, and said, Lo, this hath touched thy lips; and thine iniquity is taken away, and thy sin purged" (Isaiah 6:1-3; 5-7).

"Holy, holy, holy, is the Lord of hosts. The whole earth is full of his glory." It is rather difficult for us to comprehend someone who is truly holy. The holiness of God means He is perfect, that is, He is free from all evil. He has no lack of understanding. He knows all things. There is no spot or flaw in His will. God loves all truth and righteousness. He values purity. Not only does God have no lack of understanding, but His understanding is perfect. He is without sin, and His love is selfless.

Sometimes we are holy, but too often our holiness is merely a facade. We know what to do to appear holy. We know, for instance, that to appear holy, we ought to read the Bible, we ought to attend church, we ought to reach others with the gospel. There are many things we can do to appear holy. Unfortunately, we may do these things and still not be truly holy. You see, holiness can be separated from us. This is not true of God.

Moreover, since God is immutable or unchangeable, He can never be less holy than He is at this very minute. On the other hand, He can never be more holy than He is now.

Furthermore, God can never approve that which is unholy. If you are contemplating a course of action which you know involves sin, you can be sure God does not approve. Are there some things less evil than others? Is it better for Christians to do those rather than more evil things? On the basis of God's holiness, we must conclude Christians should do nothing that involves sin. Since God can never approve that which is unholy, we must be holy in order to merit His approval.

God can never hate in one person what He loves in another. This means if He accepts some action in me as a rightful action, He will also accept it in you.

While Christ's blood makes us acceptable to God, it is the holiness He gives us which makes us acceptable to a holy God. Christ's holiness, His righteousness is imputed to us. Therefore, God looks upon us as holy. Because God is truly holy, He continues to hate our sin, even though we are His children. Consequently, we should avoid sin.

Although sometimes we think His holiness is passive, it is actually active. God's holiness causes Him to judge and punish evil. If His holiness were not active, it might be possible for sin to remain unpunished. Since it is active, He judges and punishes sin.

The passage of Scripture with which we opened this chapter clearly indicates that God is holy. The book of Revelation states that the creatures are going to cry, "Holy, holy, holy, Lord God Almighty" (cf. Revelation 4:8). Both the Old and New Testaments state that the children of God are to be holy, as God is holy.

Not only does Scripture prove God is holy, but His creation also proves it. However, we must look at creation as it looked when it first came from the hands of the Creator, not as it is today. Man and creation as they appear today are not holy. However, the original creation was holy. The fact that God came to fellowship with Adam and Eve in the Garden of Eden implies man was a holy being. Since this is the case, it must follow that Adam and Eve, as they came from the hands of God, must have been holy. We find no indication of a need for reconciliation or sacrifice before the fall. Since man, as he came from the hands of his Creator, God, was a holy creature, God Himself must also be holy.

God's laws and judgments are also proof of His

holiness. God's law, the total standard of God, is a holy law. It is a correct law. This law, which includes the Mosaic law, is the total revelation of God's righteousness. A study of this revelation as recorded in Scripture shows He is indeed a holy God. God's Word says God will not allow sinners to come before His presence. The sinner must first take care of the sin.

Finally, we see that God's judgments are always correct. I do not know about your judgment and the punishment you mete out, but I can still remember once or twice when I as a father did not exercise correct judgment.

One day three of our children were playing in their bedroom. Things were rather quiet when all of a sudden I heard a blood-curdling scream. It sounded like someone had been killed. I jumped out of my chair and burst into the bedroom. I picked up the child closest to me and gave her a swat on the you-know-where. "What did you do?" I bellowed.

Unfortunately, I punished the wrong child. The child I had punished had been sitting calmly reading a book. It was the two in the far corner who were having the fracas. My judgment was wrong and my punishment was not holy. As a matter of fact, my punishment was wrong.

God's judgments are never wrong. They are always right. Hebrews 10:30, in effect, says, "Vengeance is mine. I will repay, saith the Lord." The word, *vengeance,* means He will vindicate His honor. He will do what is necessary for each person.

To us, vengeance means getting even with someone or maybe doing a little bit more. This is not true of God.

The greatest proof of the holiness of God is our salvation. God's holiness demanded a sacrifice adequate to take care of the problem of man's sin. Christ's death on the cross proves that God is a holy God, because only God Himself incarnate could adequately take care of the problem. Therefore, we will come to an understanding of the holiness of God only when we look at it against the backdrop of Christ's sacrifice on the cross. God's holiness demands an adequate sacrifice and since we could not pay that sacrifice, God Himself paid it.

How is His holiness manifested? God manifests His holiness by judging those who sin. He first manifested His holiness when he ejected Adam and Eve from the Garden of Eden. The very fact that God was holy necessitated their expulsion so they would not eat of the Tree of Life. If they had, they would have continued forever in their sinful state.

On the other hand, God did not simply throw Adam and Eve out, but He provided for their needs as well. We do not know all that happened, but He must have made some sort of sacrifice. It seems evident that He sacrificed an animal and gave them instructions concerning it. Thus, although His holiness caused Him to judge Adam and Eve and their sin, He provided for them.

God manifested His holiness throughout the Old Testament by judging not only sinners but the people of God as well. If His own people do not live by His standard of holiness, they must face judgment.

His dealings with the children of Israel illustrate this. Time after time they failed to live by the standard God had established. We see this especially in the Book of Judges. God brought the people into the land, but after Joshua died, they turned from God to idols. Then, because He is holy, God judged them. He allowed them to be conquered by the nations around them. When the children of Israel acknowledged their sin and repented, God forgave them. He gave them a judge and restored them to a position of peace and fellowship. However, in a few years, the cycle began again. Again, God brought judgment to bear on them.

David also illustrates this. He sinned grievously when he committed his well-known sins with Bathsheba. He murdered; he committed adultery; he coveted; and he broke just about all ten commandments. And God brought David up short. He judged him. God judged David again when, filled with pride, he disobeyed God and numbered the people of Israel to see how strong they were. He knew God did not want him to do that. Because of His holiness, God judges His own people.

God not only judges His own people, but He judges the sinner as well. Sometimes he delays His judgment; but it always comes. Habakkuk had a hard time understanding this. He could not understand how God could use a sinful nation like the Chaldeans to judge His people.

"The just shall live by his faith," God told Habakkuk (2:4). Then He might have added, "Wait! I'll judge them also."

God did judge the Chaldeans. Their civilization was totally destroyed; it ceased to exist. What God judges in one, He will also judge in another.

The Trinity provides opportunity for God to manifest His holiness. For us, a triangle indicates trouble. A triangle immediately brings to mind a third person interfering with a married couple, and this normally spells trouble. Paradoxically, this is not true of God's Trinity. There is no selfishness in the love of the Godhead because God is truly holy. God is perfect. He is unpolluted. He is free from all evil.

Once again, the condemnation of God's own Son most clearly illustrates God's holiness. The crucifixion demonstrates God's love, His grace and His mercy, but it also shows His holiness. Obviously, God did not desire to see His Son die. He did not want sin to separate Him from His only Son. However, His holiness was such that only His Son's death could adequately take care of the problem.

God's holiness makes man hate God, for he realizes he himself falls short of being holy. He knows he can never hope to meet God's standard. If we are honest with ourselves, we know we cannot even live up to what we ourselves would like to be. Although we make all kinds of resolutions, we cannot keep them for any length of time.

We say we are not going to lose our temper. It seems the moment we make that decision something happens that puts us to the test. Before we know it, we have lost our temper. We cannot measure up to the standard we set for ourselves, let alone God's standard of holiness. Because of this, man tends to turn from God and make a god to which he can measure up. I believe this is why the gods of the Greeks and the Romans were made in the image of man.

The gods all had the problems of men. The gods on Mt. Olympus were always quarreling among themselves. They always argued as to who was the greatest, the most beautiful and the most powerful. All the gods were involved in sexual immorality with one another and with men and women. Men turned from the true and holy God to their idols because they could measure up to the standard of the gods.

God's holiness causes sinners to hate holiness in other people. Why do you think the unsaved go to such lengths to involve other people in their actions? If they can persuade a child of God to commit the sins they commit, they feel they have proven God is not really a holy God.

It is important for us to realize as sinners we cannot come into His presence on our own merit. Anyone who thinks he can clearly proves he does not understand that God is a holy God. If we truly recognize God as being perfect, without spot or blemish and without evil, we will realize we can never stand in His presence on our own. Scripture tells us that at the last judgment great and mighty men of earth will cry out for the rocks to fall upon them and hide them from the face of God. Too late, they will realize they cannot stand in His presence.

If we truly understand the holiness of God, it will help us have a proper attitude toward sin. Although

God reveals His grace when He forgives our sin, we should understand that we should not go on sinning to give Him more opportunity to reveal that grace. In the Book of Romans, the Apostle Paul says, "Shall we continue in sin that grace may abound? God forbid!" Anyone who says we should continue in sin so the grace of God can be more fully manifested toward us does not understand the holiness of God. I personally question whether or not such a one really knows God at all.

God is holy and He will not encourage us to sin. He never asks us to do anything unrighteous. He never commands us to sin. He never inspires us to do evil. God hates sin and He Himself can do no evil. A proper understanding of God will lead us to avoid all sin.

On the other hand, God's holiness must be satisfied. It is not a passive thing. God's holiness is active and demands punishment for sin. Either we pay the penalty for sin or someone else must pay for it. We cannot because we are sinners. The only way the holiness of God can be satisfied is by a Mediator, and that Mediator is the Lord Jesus Christ.

While the holiness of God is a problem for the lost, it should be a comfort to those who are saved. We know we have a God who is truly worthy of our worship. We know He is the kind of God who is worthy of our service. We know He is the kind of God who will hear and answer our prayers. We know God is truly holy.

Furthermore, His holiness should make us want to be like God. We ought to have a deep desire to do

His will, to do everything we can to please Him. We ought to measure our conduct against God's standard. First Peter 1:15,16 says, "But as he which hath called you is holy, so be ye holy in all manner of conversation. Because it is written, Be ye holy; for I am holy."

8. His Justice

What is the justice of God? The justice of God is very closely related to the holiness of God. To us justice is a strict adherence to the law. That is, if we are just, we will do nothing that goes contrary to the law itself. We will follow the exact letter of the law. We will do nothing to violate that law. This may express our concept of justice in relation to man, but it cannot express our concept of justice in relationship to God. You see, there is no law by which God must abide.

It is true that God cannot in any way violate His own Being, and there is no outside standard that God can follow. That means, for all practical purposes, His justice is absolute. He is just because he is God. He will not do anything that violates any aspect of His own Being. God is righteous in and of Himself. He does nothing that is wrong. He does nothing that is evil. He does nothing out of a sense of hatred. He always acts out of the goodness of His Being. He always does that which is right for the individual. To summarize, we are saying that God is infinitely righteous of Himself. He is righteous and what He does is always just or right.

Once again, this is hard for us to comprehend. To

understand justice, we need a standard by which we can measure. The standard we use is the law. We say a person is just because he does not violate any of the laws or he treats everyone equally. To us, that's justice. Not so with God. He is infinitely righteous in Himself. This is absolute justice.

God not only has absolute justice but He also has relative justice; that is, His justice looks at the way in which God maintains Himself as a Holy One. God is not only a just God, but He is also a holy or righteous God. God deals with any violation of His holiness, and the very way in which God responds to this violation proves that He is holy and at the same time just.

God deals adequately with every violation of His holiness. He always deals with it in a way that is fair to everyone. Our problem, of course, is that we do not always recognize this. We somehow seem to think we should not be treated like everybody else. However, true justice demands equal treatment. God does this in the maintenance of His holiness. His relative justice, then, looks at that aspect of God which He Himself maintains as the Holy One against every violation of holiness. This shows that God is indeed the Holy One as well as the Just One.

It is difficult to comprehend these truths because our vision is limited; it's finite. With God it is infinite. We know that we are far from being just individuals. Therefore, a being who is infinitely just or perfect in all of His dealings with men from the standpoint of justice is beyond our comprehension. Yet, we need to recognize that God is such a being.

Is there proof of the justice of God? Numerous passages refer to God's justice, but I would like to direct your attention to Romans 3:21-28:

> But now the righteousness of God without the law is manifested, being witnessed by the law and the prophets: Even the righteousness of God which is by faith of Jesus Christ unto all and upon all them that believe: for there is no difference: For all have sinned, and come short of the glory of God; Being justified freely by his grace through the redemption that is in Christ Jesus: Whom God hath set forth to be a propitiation through faith in his blood, to declare his righteousness for the remission of sins that are past, through the forbearance of God; To declare, I say, at this time his righteousness: that he might be just, and the justifier of him which believeth in Jesus. Where is boasting then? It is excluded. By what law? of works? Nay: but by the law of faith. Therefore we conclude that a man is justified by faith without the deeds of the law.

This passage of Scripture concerns God and His relationship to the lost. It says that God is a righteous God and that all men have sinned and come short of the glory of God. Men are in trouble, they must come before a righteous and holy God. But God is also just. The Bible assures us that God can forgive men's sins on the basis of Christ's sacrifice. Because of this work of Jesus Christ, He can declare them righteous and forgive their sin, sins that are in the past and sins that are occurring in the present.

Verse 26 says that God is just: "That he might be just, and the justifier of him which believeth in Jesus." To be a just God means that all of the sins of man must be adequately punished. God can be just because the penalty for our sins was placed upon the Lord Jesus Christ. There is no one who can say God is not just.

God's dealings with Israel demonstrated God's justice. God always had to have a basis for forgiving Israel's sins. The passage we looked at in Romans says that God was just in forgiving sins in the past through His forbearance. He waited until the Lord Jesus Christ came. The work on the cross not only adequately took care of the sins which have been committed since His death, but it took care of the sins prior to His death. Therefore, God was just when He declared the sins of Israel forgiven. If Israel did not come on the proper basis, that is, if they did not bring a proper sacrifice and if they did not confess their sins, God also dealt with them. Sin does not go unpunished.

Because He does not always judge immediately, we may think God does not judge sin. God does not view time as we do. We may sin today and God may give us ample opportunity to deal with it, but He eventually judges if we do not judge ourselves. This is clearly seen in the case of Israel. God was fair in His dealings with the Israelites. He was just, and He did judge their sins.

We also see proof for God's justice in His plan of salvation. Once again, all of the attributes of God must work together. We cannot overemphasize one at the expense of another. While God is a God of love, He also is a God of justice. This means that sin must be punished. Since man could not pay the penalty himself, the goodness of God, the grace of God, the mercy of God and the love of God caused Him to provide a way. That way, as we have said many times already, was through the death of Jesus Christ. When by faith we accept Jesus Christ, God declares us justified. God is perfectly just in doing so since Christ paid for our sins. The justice of God has been satisfied. He can be just and still justify us as sinners. The justice of God as seen in the plan of salvation is one of the greatest proofs of His justice.

Although the plan of salvation is the greatest manifestation of God's justice, it was unfair to Jesus Christ. Christ did not have to become the sin-bearer. He willingly went to the cross and bore your sins and mine as evidence of God's justice and the need to punish sin. On that basis, then, God can declare us righteous, as we read in Romans 3:26. Jesus Christ has paid the penalty for our sins.

It is hard for us to understand the justice of God. We can understand that He is loving, holy and righteous. However, we cannot emphasize His love to the extent that it overshadows His justice. As a matter of fact, we will never fully understand the love of God until we understand that God is a holy and righteous God. It is only when we understand that, because of His holiness, God was forced to send His Son to die on the cross that we can understand His love.

Many years ago in New England the church preached what was called the "halfway covenant." They believed that children born into Christian families were in some special relationship with God. According to their teaching, that child would somehow just grow in the faith and become a full mature Christian without a personal commitment to God. As a result of this teaching, the church became filled with people who really did not know God. They became more and more lethargic, less inclined to serve God.

Then a few individuals like Jonathan Edwards and George Whitfield burst on the scene and completely changed the outlook of the New England church. They preached the holiness of God and the justice of God. When people realized that God was indeed a holy God, that He could not allow sin to stand in His presence, that He was a just God, that He would adequately deal with every act of sin, they understood their desperate need.

Against this background of holiness and justice, the love of God became truly evident. Literally thousands and tens of thousands were swept into the church of God. Earlier, the church had emphasized the love of God to the extent that men no longer appreciated it. As a result, they ignored the provision that God had made for them in Jesus Christ.

How is God's justice seen? Since God is the ruler over all, He establishes a moral, just government. We see this illustrated when God gave the Law. The

Law for the children of Israel was more than just a standard of conduct before God. The Law of Moses was also to be the standard for their government. It was to be the law of the land. It was to establish a moral, just government. Unfortunately, the people of Israel never really carried out the commands of the law. If they had, they would have had the kind of government God wanted them to have.

We also see that God manifests His justice in connection with His rewards and punishment. God always rewards and punishes correctly. It is difficult for us to be just in all our dealings. The legislatures face this problem when they attempt to establish laws governing crime. One judge may give an offender a slap on the wrist and give the criminal only a probationary sentence while another judge, for the exact crime, will sentence another to prison for a long time. We say that is not just, that one of those criminals did not receive what he deserved. We may not be sure which person received unjust treatment, but we say justice has miscarried. God always rewards and punishes correctly for any violation of His standard. We see His justice in this respect.

We also see God's justice when He rewards the righteous. Contrary to what many believe, God will not reward us for what we ourselves do. Scripture teaches that God will reward us for allowing the Holy Spirit to do the work through us. Since we do not really do anything but allow the Spirit of God to work through us, God can reward us and be perfectly just. He is not really rewarding us for what we have done; He is rewarding us for what *He* has done.

Therefore, there is no thought of merit on our part.

If I receive a reward, I can only say it is because of the grace of God, who has given me such a reward. I cannot boast or brag about any reward that I receive. Neither can you; it comes as a result of our allowing God to work through us. He can be truly just when He rewards us at the judgment seat of Christ.

The penalty God sets for sin also illustrates His justice. These penalties are really designed to promote righteousness and holiness. God does not arbitrarily judge and punish us. He does not desire to see us suffer. He brings judgment upon us to make us aware of our sin, to stop our sinning and cause us to deal with that sin, and thus become righteous and holy. The penalties are designed to help us understand where we have failed and to show us the kind of people we ought to be.

What should this mean to us? We ought to worship such a God, accepting that He is a just God. He will treat everyone correctly with respect to his or her sin. His judgment of sin and distribution of rewards are right. It ought to cause us to recognize what kind of a being He is. Do you know of anyone who even approaches this kind of standard? No one even comes close.

Knowing that God is just also ought to encourage and comfort us. Do you realize that there is absolutely no possibility of favoritism with God? Do you realize that because God is just, He will treat you exactly like He treats His Son, Jesus Christ? Whatever He does for Christ, He will do for you.

Because He is just, He has no favorites.

Obviously, when we talk about being treated equally, we are talking about born-again believers. However, the same holds true for the sinner. One sinner will be treated just as fairly as another. Nevertheless, God will condemn the sinner for rejecting the sacrifice of Jesus Christ. The sinner who rejects that sacrifice commits the only sin which cannot be forgiven. He has rejected the only sacrifice which can take care of the problem. God will judge the sinner on the basis of the light he had and how often he rejected it, but He will judge him. Although the sinner is already condemned because of his sin, God will justify the sinner if he puts his faith in Jesus Christ.

It should encourage and comfort us to understand that God does not play favorites. It also ought to cause us to value our salvation even more. Considering His holiness and His justice ought to cause us to pour out our hearts in thanksgiving. You see, there is no hope for us outside the Lord Jesus Christ. In no way could we adequately satisfy the demands of a holy, righteous God. The only thing that God could justly do would be to condemn us for our sins. Yet, the exact opposite is true because of what Christ has done. Christ paid the penalty and now we are declared justified. God looks upon us as though we had never sinned. Do you really understand what it means to have a just God? Does it make any difference to your life to know that this is the kind of God you have? Does it make you appreciate and value your salvation more? Our God is a just God.

9. His Love

Although many theologians consider the love of God as a part of the goodness of God, I think it is significant enough that it should be discussed separately. Because some theologians discuss love and goodness separately, I think I can safely follow their example.

First John 4:7-10,16 is the basis for our consideration.

> Beloved, let us love one another: for love is of God; and every one that loveth is born of God, and knoweth God. He that loveth not knoweth not God; for God is love. In this was manifested the love of God toward us, because that God sent his only begotten Son into the world, that we might live through him. Herein is love, not that we loved God, but that he loved us, and sent his Son to be the propitiation for our sins . . . And we have known and believed the love that God hath to us. God is love; and he that dwelleth in love dwelleth in God, and God in him.

Love is what causes God to communicate Himself

to man. Love is the goodness of God revealed to man. God's love causes Him to want others to be like Him and to be where He is. The Greek language has three words for *love*. The word, *eros*, which refers to sensual intoxication or sexual love is not used in the New Testament. For the Greeks this erotic love was the supreme form of ecstasy. It led to the original form of eroticism in pagan religions. This kind of experience was the highest form of worship the Greeks could have. In the Greek context, erotic love is a universal, nonselective love.

A second word for love is *phileo*. It looks at love of a friend for a friend. In Greek usage it could be the love of the gods for a man. This kind of love is optional. It is not something that you just have to have, but it is something that you may have. It is not an impulse or intoxication or something that must be satisfied. This kind of friendly love, the concern of one person for another, can be avoided.

The third word for love is *agape*. In older Greek usage agape is a weak and uncertain word. We cannot find too many uses of it in literature that is contemporaneous with the New Testament. There are, however, enough secular uses of it that we can determine its meaning. Scripture, particularly, gives a clear definition.

Agape love in Scripture is love given as the result of a free and decisive act that is determined by the one who does the loving. Actually, it depicts an individual who is higher looking down on one who is on a lower level, raising the one on the lower level and making him equal with the one who is doing the raising. It means to show concern. It means to be active in manifesting this love to others. It is an attitude, not an emotion or feeling.

God's love causes Him to want others to be like Him and to be where He is. In order to do that, He manifests His love particularly in the Person and work of the Lord Jesus Christ. Through faith in the work of Christ, we as individuals experience the love of God. We can actually be brought from this lower level up to a level where we can have fellowship with the Almighty God and become like Him. God's love causes Him to desire to communicate Himself, to bring others where He is and to make them like Himself.

We must recognize that the love of God is infinite. That means there is no beginning and no end to it. It has always been. It is not something that starts and stops. His love does not change. We do not think of love as eternal. We are accustomed to hearing about people falling in and out of love. One moment they are in love with one person and the next moment they are no longer in love with that person but are in love with another. By our use of the word love, we tend to make it a very light thing. We see something and we say, "Oh, my, I just love that," or "Don't you love this outfit?" or "Don't you love our new car?"

We actually mean, "I really think this is nice," or "Don't you think my outfit looks nice?" or "Isn't this a nice car?" Not only does God's love not change, but it is free from all selfishness or partiality. When we think of a triangle involving people, we think of trouble. On the other hand, a triangle in connection with God is the best example of the selflessness of the love of God.

God the Father loves God the Son equally with God the Holy Spirit. On the other hand, God the Son loves God the Father the same as He loves God the Holy Spirit. The Holy Spirit loves God the Father and the Son equally. There is no partiality there. Each loves each person in the Trinity the same.

The love of God is pure and holy. We must keep the attributes of God in balance. God can never love that which is unholy or impure. He loves that which is holy or right and good. So God's love is poured out upon that which is a reflection of the kind of being He is.

God loves the sinner, but what God loves is the person of the sinner. He does not love the acts of sin. God's love is for that which is pure and holy.

Do we have any proof for this characteristic of God? First John says, "God is love." Many other portions of Scripture declare God is indeed love. John 3:16 says, "For God so loved the world that he gave his only begotten Son." Over and over the Scriptures testify to God's love.

The creation of God also is evidence that God is love. Why did God create man, the world and the universe? There are many reasons, but certainly He created them to manifest His love. God was not satisfied to merely exercise His love within the Trinity. He desired to pour out His love upon men. Consequently, He loved man, knowing full well before

He ever created man that he would sin. God knew man would need mercy and grace as well as love. Nevertheless, God created. This gave Him an opportunity to manifest His love. God's provision and care for all living things clearly indicates the love of God.

The love of God is not only manifested in His creation, and in His care and concern for creation, but the greatest example of this love is seen in salvation. God is not compelled to do anything for us. We are sinners. God would be perfectly just to simply condemn us for our sins. However, being the kind of God He is, a God of mercy, a God of grace, and a God of love, He provided salvation.

We can never hope to fully understand the love of God until it is placed against His holiness and His justice. God is a holy God, and He must punish sin. He is a just God and will adequately deal with sin. Since we could not pay for the sin ourselves, God, out of love, provided the way of salvation. As a result, we can come by faith and accept Jesus Christ. Having done that, we become children of God (I John 3:1,2).

On the other hand, the unbeliever should recognize that although God is a God of love, He will judge the unbeliever. He may not judge the sinner immediately, but judgment will come. God is holy, righteous and just, and these qualities must be satisfied. Either the sinner comes and accepts the manifestation of God's love by placing his faith in the Lord Jesus Christ, or he faces judgment. God's love caused Him to make a way of escape. Each person must personally appropriate that way of escape. Otherwise, he stands alone.

God's love is completely selfless. Human love is not always selfless. The love my wife and I had for each other before we had children was rather selfish. We were wrapped up and concerned with each other. When our first child was born, it was a rude shock to find that I had to share my wife's affection with someone else. True, I loved that child, but if I were honest, I must admit there was an element of jealousy toward that little bit of humanity. Once I alone held that special place in my wife's affection, but now I had to make room for someone else.

God loves all individuals equally. Children find it difficult to understand that parents love each of their children equally. I cannot speak from experience for I happen to be the youngest child; however, I understand many older children find it difficult to really understand that their parents still love them when a new baby is born into the family. They cannot understand how parents could still love them as they loved them before.

Those of us who are parents understand that the love just expands. There is no diminishing of our love toward our older children when another arrives. The love just encompasses them all. This is true of the love of God, as well. God loves all people equally. If God is truly immutable, or unchangeable, His love can never change.

God also loves His creation and the rational creatures that are in it. However, He loves the rational creatures in a way that He does not love the creation itself. He must love the creation in some respect because He continues to care and provide for it. However, the love of God which motivates Him to want us to be like Himself cannot be poured out upon the inanimate creation.

God does not withdraw His love from men. Adam and Eve sinned and lost fellowship with God, but that did not change God's love toward them. He still loved them. Because He loved them, He provided for them. The same is true with us today. God does not withdraw His love from His children. Rather, because He loves us with an unchangeable love, He will provide for our needs.

Does He cease loving us when He judges us? We cannot oppose the love of God to the judgment of God nor His chastisement. Although God loves us, it does not mean that He will withhold His judgment from us. The very fact that He does judge us is proof of His love (cf. Hebrews 12).

A study of the Scriptures shows that His love is manifested toward His own people. In the Old Testament, especially after the nation Israel came into existence, God manifested His love toward His people.

In the New Testament, especially in the Epistles, we see that the love of God is poured out primarily upon the church, that is, the body of believers. Nonetheless, we still see the love of God with respect to all men in general.

While He does love the church in a special way, He also loves all people. We know this from such passages of Scripture as John 3:16. "For God so loved the world that he gave his only begotten Son . . . ." The world is that system which crucified the Lord Jesus Christ. God loved that world and Christ died for that world.

How does God show His love? His love is shown most fully in salvation. We looked at this quite extensively in connection with the proof of His love. Because He loves sinners, He gives them mercy and grace.

God shows His love in providing for His own. God is under no compulsion to meet our needs, but because He loves us, we can come to the throne of grace to find help in time of need. The fact that God continues to meet my needs day by day in spite of my unfaithfulness, in spite of my sin and failures, proves God loves me.

His chastisement also proves His love. Chastisement or discipline is something we really do not like. We read in Hebrews 12:5,6: "And ye have forgotten the exhortation which speaketh unto you as unto children, My son, despise not thou the chastening of the Lord, nor faint when thou art rebuked of him. For whom the Lord loveth he chasteneth, and scourgeth every son whom he receiveth.' "

The chastening that God pours out upon us is proof that He loves us and cares for us. Many believe parents who love their children will not discipline them; they will simply let them go their own way. This is not true. We prove our love to our children by correcting them, by teaching them standards of conduct. Furthermore, this instruction helps them cope with relationships and circumstances throughout their lifetimes.

Discipline, then, proves our concern for them. If we do not establish guidelines, they are apt to believe we are unconcerned. Just as the discipline of our children shows our love, so God's discipline shows His love for us.

According to Isaiah 63:9, His love is manifested in sharing affliction with His own. When we accept Jesus Christ, God Himself in the person of the Holy Spirit indwells us. This means that God Himself is in every experience through which we go. He shares all our difficulties, troubles and trials. He knows. He is there and He shares them with us because He loves us.

God shows His love by forgiving the sins of the believer. He would not have to forgive our sin, but He does. According to I John 1:9, "If we confess our sins, He is faithful and just to forgive us our sins, and to cleanse us from all unrighteousness." Why does He forgive? He does it because He loves us and wants us to experience His forgiveness.

What should this mean to us? It should cause us to bow down and worship Him. He does not demand of us that which we cannot do or give. God loves us so He does for us all that we need. God's love ought to cause us to respond with love for Him.

If we truly love God, it will have an impact upon us and we will love one another. Those who observed the early church said, "Behold, how they love each other." Love characterized that early church. As brothers and sisters in Christ we also ought to have a love for one another. That kind of love puts a brother's welfare on par or above our own. We should desire to do all we can for him as God does for us.

If we truly love God and each other, there will be a love for the lost because we love what God loves. Since God loves the lost and wants all people to come to Him, I should do all I can to bring the lost person to Him. I should want them to love God as I do. What does it mean to you to have a God of love?

10. His Mercy

The attributes of God all work together. One cannot be in conflict with another. If they were, God would not truly be God. He would not be perfect. He would not be what Scripture declares He is. His justice cannot oppose His mercy. The mercy of God never violates the justice of God. Some people emphasize one at the expense of another, but they should not.

The mercy of God is bountiful. God is not forced to be merciful to us. He is merciful simply because He desires to exercise His mercy. God is not compelled to be merciful, yet He is.

The mercy of God endures forever. God did not *become* merciful when a need for mercy arose. Mercy has always been a part of His personality. It is true, He could not show mercy until someone needed mercy. Nevertheless, He did not then become merciful. God is immutable, and there can be no change in His essence or basic personality. This means that mercy always has been a part of His nature, however, He could manifest mercy only after He had created the universe and the world.

Psalm 136 emphasizes the fact that His mercy is eternal. "O give thanks unto the Lord; for he is good: for his mercy endureth for ever. O give thanks unto the God of gods: for his mercy endureth for ever. O give thanks to the Lord of lords: for his mercy endureth for ever" (verses 1-3). Notice that each of the twenty-six verses of this Psalm ends with the phrase, "for his mercy endureth for ever." The repetition of this phrase emphasizes the importance of the concept that God always has had mercy and will always exercise it.

The nature of mercy is that it is always undeserved. We do not deserve mercy from the hand of God. What we deserve is judgment. However, being a God of mercy, God pours out mercy upon us.

We cannot oppose mercy in the Old Testament to love and grace in the New. Although the Old Testament refers to the concept of mercy far more than the New Testament does, God is the same in all ages. We must keep the immutability of God in mind in this context as well. Since God cannot change, He is merciful in the Old Testament and He is also a merciful God in the New. If this were not true it would contradict His immutability. God is not more merciful now than He was in the past. He will not be more merciful in the future than He is now.

Mercy is the tender compassion of God. It is the goodness of God shown to those in need or in distress, be he saint or sinner. God shows His mercy by moving to meet human need. Remember, if there is no guilt or despair, if there is no need, then there is no necessity for mercy. However, there is need. Man must have help.

What proof do we have? Scripture frequently

mentions the mercy of God. We find this concept not only in Psalm 136 to which we referred earlier, but we also find it in other Psalms. For example, Psalm 23:6 says, "Surely goodness and mercy shall follow me all the days of my life: and I will dwell in the house of the Lord for ever."

According to Psalm 57:10, God gives His mercy without measure, and in Psalm 106:1, we read that it is enduring. Exodus 20:2-6 and Deuteronomy 7:9 indicate that the mercy is poured out on those who fear Him.

In the New Testament the mercy of God is often connected with grace and peace. We find this particularly true in the salutations of some of the Epistles. For example, in I and II Timothy, the Apostle Paul requests grace, mercy and peace for Timothy.

God's concern for the works of His hands also gives support for His mercy. He particularly manifests this concern to man, but He also manifests it to the whole of His creative works. The mercy of God is really the compassion of God. He is merciful toward sinner and saint alike. If it were not for God's mercy, all men would be consumed by His wrath.

This would be especially true for the sinner. However, because God is merciful, He withholds His judgment and meets men's needs even though they do not deserve it. The mercy of God looks at God's being good or bountiful to man as a criminal. That is, man is a criminal, worthy only of judgment, but God in His mercy withholds that judgment and gives mankind the opportunity to repent. This demonstrates His tender compassion. It is the goodness of God that is shown to those who are in need or in distress whether they are sinners or saints. It is the exercise of His goodness toward His creatures.

Let me emphasize, we must not set God's mercy up in opposition to His justice. God is not only holy and righteous, but He is just. He can also be merciful because of the Lord Jesus Christ. He can extend His bounty toward His creatures because He knows that Jesus Christ in His sacrificial death satisfies God's justice. Although God is a just God, He is a merciful God as well and we can experience that mercy.

God shows His mercy by His concern for His works. He really is concerned about His creation. For example, in Psalm 145:9 we read, "The Lord is good to all: and his tender mercies are over all his works." This Psalm states we can see God's mercy in His care and concern for the works of His hands. Mankind and the world in general has not been judged, and the final problem of sin has not been taken care of because God is merciful and in His mercy, He holds judgment. He gives man opportunity to come to Him through faith in Jesus Christ. If this were not true, God would simply conclude the matter of sin and its contamination of the world by judging sin. Instead, He waits, and He continues to pour mercy out upon His works. The very continuance of the heaven and earth is an indication of the mercy of God.

God also shows His mercy by not dealing with sin

105

immediately. When our original parents sinned, God could have dealt with that sin at once, but instead, He made provision for their sin. If God judged sin immediately, as He could, all individuals would be taken at once in death. According to Romans, "All have sinned, and come short of the glory of God," and "The wages of sin is death" (Romans 3:23; 6:23). This includes all of us. If God did not withhold His judgment, we would all die.

God especially withholds judgment in the life of the child of God. God does not judge us immediately when we are involved in sin; He waits to give us opportunity to deal with sin on our own. He allows the Holy Spirit to convict us so we can judge ourselves.

The greatest illustration of God's mercy is His provision of salvation. Once again, God was under no compulsion to make provision for our sins, but in mercy and tender compassion He recognized that we had no hope. There was absolutely nothing we could do to meet our need. As far as God is concerned, we are criminals. We are guilty and there is nothing we can do.

However, because He is merciful, God meets our needs. In so doing, He provides salvation for us. His mercy worked out the plan by which He could be just and at the same time demonstrate His concern for us. That plan is salvation.

He not only worked out the plan, but He uses it. It is one thing to have a plan, but it is another thing to implement the plan and see that it operates. God not only planned salvation, but He actually saves the lost. God through the Holy Spirit worked in our hearts while we were sinners, causing us to see our desperate need. He caused us to respond to the preaching of the gospel. Thus, God's mercy is most fully seen in actually saving the lost. We see His mercy demonstrated as the Holy Spirit causes the sinner to see his need and, upon seeing that need, accept Jesus Christ as his Saviour.

God's mercy is the basis for help to live the Christian life. Hebrews 4:15-16 says:

> For we have not an high priest who cannot be touched with the feeling of our infirmities; but was in all points tempted like as we are, yet without sin. Let us therefore come boldly unto the throne of grace, that we may obtain mercy, and find grace to help in time of need.

The writer encourages us to come boldly to the throne of grace to find mercy. Why? Why should we come without fear? It is because we know our God is merciful. We know He will meet our need. God shows His mercy in His invitation as well as in His response to us when we come.

What should this mean to us? Once again, it ought to cause us to worship and praise our God because He is merciful. The gods of the pagans are cruel. They demand the best.

Their cruelty is illustrated in the *Iliad* and *Odyssey* as the Greek fleet sailed to Troy to beseige it. Because the winds were blowing from the wrong direction, Agamemnon, the leader of the fleet, believed some god was against him. He sent home a message asking that his oldest daughter be sent to him. When she came, he sacrificed her to his gods. Because the winds changed and blew from the West, Agamemnon was satisfied the gods had accepted his offering. The fleet sailed to Troy and eventually captured it. Agamemnon's god was a cruel god. In contrast, our God is merciful, meeting our needs. He deserves our praise.

We ought to be aware that mercy is available. We ought to come for mercy when we sin. Because God is merciful, He will respond with grace and forgive our sins.

God's mercy should cause us to show mercy to others. We are to manifest the nature of our God. We are to make other people understand the kind of God we have. We can never hope to show people that God is a God of mercy unless we ourselves exercise the gift of mercy. Mercy is one fruit of the Spirit listed in Galatians 5:22. We ought to exercise this gift.

God is truly a God of mercy.

11. His Grace

The grace of God is revealed only in Scripture. It is not revealed in nature. Contrary to what we tend to think, the grace of God is not the same as the mercy or love of God. They all arise out of the goodness of God, but are not really the same. Ephesians 2:4-6 shows that love, mercy and grace are different.

But God, who is rich in mercy, for his great love wherewith he loved us, Even when we were dead in sins, hath quickened [made us alive] us together with Christ, (by grace ye are saved); And hath raised us up together, and made us sit together in heavenly places in Christ Jesus.

In these verses it is clear that mercy, grace and love are three separate things. As we consider these attributes or characteristics of God, we see that this is true.

Mercy is the compassion of God that caused Him to provide a Saviour for all men. Love is the motivating factor back of all God does in saving a soul. Grace for the lost is seen only in the act of salvation. After that, grace is manifested toward the child of God alone. Grace is what God is free to do and does for the lost after Christ has died in his behalf.

Once the lost person accepts Jesus Christ, he is no longer lost; he is a child of God. As a result, all of the grace God bestows upon that individual is grace bestowed upon a saved person. Grace, therefore, is basically for the child of God.

The mercy of God and the love of God are freely bestowed upon all people, saved and unsaved alike. The mercy of God is what keeps God from judging sinners immediately, giving them a chance to repent. The mercy of God is what causes the rain to fall upon the just and the unjust alike. The love of God, again, is manifested toward all men. John 3:16 says, "God so loved the world . . . ." This was the world which hated Christ and crucified Him.

As we have seen, God is a holy, righteous God. He is also a just God. God cannot do what He might desire to do for the lost if it offends any of His other attributes. So it is not until all the claims of God against the sinner have been satisfied that God can really do what He wants to do. That's where grace comes in. God's claims against the sinner are satisfied on the basis of the work of Jesus Christ. When the sinner acknowledges that work, the grace of God saves him and then continues to provide for his needs.

When God is released from His holy demands against the sinner by the sacrifice of Christ and by that sacrifice having been accepted, then God's love is not satisfied until He has done all He can for that person. When the sinner accepts that work of Christ, he is declared justified. Then God can bestow His grace upon him.

Romans 3:24 says, "Being justified freely by his grace through the redemption that is in Christ Jesus." Being justified means that God looks upon us as though we had never sinned, but it is even more than that. It means then that when we have been justified, God will do everything for us that He promised to do. It really means that He will make us like our Lord Jesus Christ, His Son. It says, for example, in Romans 8:29, "For whom he did foreknow, he also did predestinate to be conformed to the image of his Son, that he [Christ] might be the firstborn among many brethren." Therefore, when God declares us justified on the basis of His grace, that grace continues to operate in our lives to make us exactly like Jesus Christ.

Second Corinthians 8:9 says, "For ye know the grace of our Lord Jesus Christ, that, though he was rich, yet for your sakes he became poor, that ye through his poverty might be rich." We see the grace of God proven and manifested in His working for us. God not only provides for our salvation, but takes us from a state of absolute poverty and helplessness and makes us rich in Jesus Christ. The grace of God is the basis for our justification.

God also manifests His grace so He can accomplish for us all that He said He would do. When released from His righteous demands with respect to the sinner, God is free to satisfy His love. He will not be satisfied until He does all He possibly can for the sinner. Grace is what He does and will do for those who trust Christ. Please note that if it is truly grace, no works of our own can enter in. The moment works enter in, it is no longer grace. Grace calls for confidence in the One who saves. If we do not have complete confidence in the salvation Christ provides, if we attempt to *do* anything, it is no longer grace, but works. This is emphasized over and over in the Scriptures.

Grace makes possible the only salvation now offered to men. You cannot get to God and be accepted by Him by doing things yourself. The only way you can come into the presence of God and have fellowship with Him is on the basis of the grace of God.

Grace also provides security for His children because God continues to do what is needed for them. Romans 5:1, 2 says:

> Therefore being justified by faith, we have peace with God through our Lord Jesus Christ: By whom also we have access by faith into this grace wherein we stand, and rejoice in hope of the glory of God.

Not only are we saved through grace, but we also stand in grace. You see, if it were not for the graciousness of God bestowed upon me day by day, I would have absolutely no hope, even as a child of God. All too often we rebel against God and it is only because of the grace of God that we continue to stand in a relationship with Him. It does not depend upon what we have done. If it depended upon what we had done, we would lose that relationship. It depends upon God's grace and, therefore, we are secure.

God also manifests His grace by directing and guiding us. The Apostle Paul, writing in I Corinthians 15:9-10, says:

> For I am the least of the apostles, that am not meet to be called an apostle, because I persecuted the church of God. But by the grace of God I am what I am: and his grace which was bestowed upon me was not in vain; but I laboured more abundantly than they all: yet not I, but the grace of God which was with me.

God guided, strengthened and empowered Paul by the grace of God, and certainly this can be true of all of us as well.

In looking at my own life and my own experience, I can see how grace operated in my life. He guided me and kept me from making even more serious errors and prevented me from committing more grievous sins than what I have. I can see the grace of God in my life and I am sure if you, as a child of God, look at your own life, you can see God's grace in yours. He directs, guides and provides. The grace of God provides everything for us. It actually provides a new motive for living. Paul says in Romans 6:1, 2: "What shall we say then? Shall we continue in sin, that grace may abound? God forbid. How shall we, that are dead to sin, live any longer therein?"

Some who claim to be children of God contend the Christian ought to continue to sin because, as he continues to sin, he experiences the grace of God even more fully because God continues to forgive. A person who says this and believes it does not fully understand the grace of God. You see, God's grace gives you another motive for living. It is not that you want to experience more and more grace through His forgiveness, but because you have experienced grace, you want to please Him. Rather than committing the worst sins so you can experience His forgiveness, you ought to do the exact opposite. You ought to pray that God by His grace will keep you from sinning, any kind of sin, gross or not.

In one sense, when we are saved, we have experienced as much of the fullness of God's grace as we can ever experience. The child of God does not need additional sin to prove God's grace. We know God is gracious because He saved us. So for the individual to say, "I'm going to continue to live in sin so I can experience the grace of God," simply means he does not know God as a holy, righteous God. If he did, he would never talk like that. That is what some of the people in Rome were saying. The Holy Spirit, through Paul, says, "God forbid!" He uses one of the strongest terms to express this. God is a gracious God but you should not trespass upon His grace. God will forgive us as Christians when we sin, but we ought not to deliberately sin. No way should we sin deliberately.

We cannot earn merit with God. God rewards us or gives us what He wants to give simply because He is a gracious God. There is nothing we can do to earn merit or favor with God. However, Scripture teaches that the believer will also stand before the judgment seat of Christ to receive rewards for what we have done in the flesh. Actually, we are going to receive rewards, not for what we have done in our own strength, but what we have allowed God through the power of the Holy Spirit to do through us.

If I preach and teach in my own strength, if I do it because I am the significant one, I will receive no reward. God will reward me for my faithfulness in teaching only if I yield myself to the Holy Spirit and allow Him to work through me to accomplish His will. There is no merit on my part. Scripture clearly teaches that God gives us a reward only because He wants to. That's grace.

Romans 4:4 says, "Now to him that worketh is the reward not reckoned of grace, but of debt." Paul further says, "For if by one man's offence death reigned by one; much more they which receive abundance of grace and of the gift of righteousness shall reign in life by one, Jesus Christ . . . Moreover the law entered, that the offence might abound. But where sin abounded, grace did much more abound" (Romans 5:17, 20).

We simply receive grace upon grace from God. There is nothing we can do to earn anything from God. God gives us what He gives because He is Graciousness.

Let me again refer to the illustration I used in Chapter 6. Suppose I assigned a paper to my Hermeneutics class. "I know you are busy," I would tell the students, "and that you are probably not quite capable yet of answering this the way I want it. Here is the paper I have written on this subject. Take this copy and simply put your name on the paper and turn it back to me. I'll give you the grade. Now, obviously, since I have written the paper, I will give each of you an 'A.' It's not my paper; it's yours because it has your name on it."

That's grace. However, suppose one student says, "No, that's not right. I can't accept that. I'm going to write the paper myself."

He writes the paper himself but he leaves out some important points in the discussion. After reading the paper, I grade him on the basis, not of what I have done, but what he has done and he fails. That is the difference between grace and works. God rewards us simply because He desires to.

Grace teaches us what we should do and gives us the power to do it. Look at Romans 6:14, 15 once again. Grace provides even the way we are to live.

God cannot withhold grace from the child of God who sins. Although He may judge the child of God, He continues to be gracious. His grace cannot decrease. It cannot produce a debt. God's grace does not put us under obligation to Him. It cannot pay a just debt. The grace of God is never an overpayment of debt. It is never involved in dealing with the sins of the unsaved. The only time the grace of God is involved with the unsaved at all is when that person comes and accepts the work of Jesus Christ on the cross. It is the mercy of God that withholds the judgment of God on the lost, not the grace of God. The grace of God begins with the act of salvation and continues in the life of the child of God.

Since God is gracious, we ought to accept His grace. Christians have difficulty graciously accepting what God does for us. Perhaps it is because it is difficult for us to simply take from someone else.

We, of course, ought also to be gracious people. As we experience the grace of God, certainly we ought to show it toward others. Far too often we do not manifest that characteristic of our God. Possibly, it is because we do not know enough about God. Yet, all Christians have experienced the grace of God. We ought, then, to be gracious as well.

When we understand that God pours out grace upon grace, that His grace leads Him to do all that His love motivates Him to do, we ought to worship such a God. There is no God like Him.

At the same time we ought not to presume upon the grace of God. We should keep this attribute in view of all the other attributes of God. We ought not, for example, emphasize the grace of God to such an extent that we forget about His holiness. We should not continue to live in sin. Certainly, the sinner outside of Christ should accept God's grace.

Our God is a God of grace.

12. His Truth

Actually, God's truth includes more than we commonly think of as truthfulness. Theologians list this attribute under different titles. Berkhoff, for example, calls it the veracity of God.

When the Lord Jesus met with His disciples in the upper room near the end of His earthly ministry, Thomas asked Him, "Lord, we know not whither [where] thou goest; and how can we know the way?"

Jesus answered, "I am the way, the truth, and the life: No man cometh unto the Father, but by me" (John 14:5,6).

In Romans 3:4 the writer says, "Let God be true, but every man a liar."

When we say God is a God of truth, we are saying God is faithful; He is loyal; He is constant; He is reliable; there is no change in Him. All of these characteristics could be used to describe His faithfulness. Faithfulness reveals Him as One who is concerned. As far as the facts are concerned, God is always correct. From this standpoint, we can say He is always truthful. He never lies. He always tells the truth. There is no error in what He says or does. We could also say that He always conforms to a proper form or standard. Thus, He is truthfulness itself or

He is always true.

Furthermore, God always affirms or supports that which is true. While God may permit a lie to continue and progress, He does not advance it. He advances only what is true.

God always abides by His promises. In this respect He is true to Himself; He is true to His word. This is true whether His promises are threats or whether they are blessings. God always remains true to His promises.

God's truthfulness involves the widest meaning that we can attach to truthfulness. In God we have realized all that God should be. He is true in this respect. He is, as a matter of fact, truth. As far as the Godhead is concerned, God is all that God should be. This is especially true of Him as contrasted to other gods. They are false gods. We do not find in them all that God ought to be. In God, however, we find all the perfections we normally would expect to find in a supreme being. On the other hand, false gods always have limitations.

What God reveals about Himself is reliable. We may depend on His revelation. This looks at what we call "ethical truth." He is what He says He is. He does not lie about Himself. He measures up to what we would call the ethical standard of truth.

God knows things as they really are. This could be called logical truth. We, on the other hand, do not always know things as they are. We may think we do, but our understanding may be deficient in some point. This is not true of God. The truthfulness of God encompasses all that we customarily think of as being truth, whether it is in the area of ethics, morality or logic. God is truth.

To summarize and define God's truthfulness we could say God's truth is seen in the perfection of His being. He is the perfect answer to the concept of God. He is completely reliable in His revelation and He sees things as they really are.

Scripture, of course, supports the fact that God is truth. To find references which confirm this, we need only check a concordance for words like faith, loyalty, truth or truthfulness. A few of the many passages which support His truthfulness are Numbers 23:19; Exodus 34:6; Psalm 25:10; Isaiah 65:16; John 14:6; John 17:3; Hebrews 6:18; and I John 5:20.

God's actions also prove His truthfulness. For example, when Noah built an altar to God after the Flood, God put His rainbow in the sky as a sign that He would never again let the world perish in a worldwide flood. God has been faithful in keeping that promise. He has been true. What He said, He has done. After a shower, the rainbow in the sky reminds us of God's faithfulness. His actions clearly prove that He is truthful.

His revelation also proves His faithfulness. When we read the Word of God and respond to its message with an act of faith, we find God always performs what He has said He will do. God has said He will save a person when that person by faith puts his trust in Jesus Christ. If God were not a truthful God, this might not always occur. However, anyone who has taken this step can verify that statement. So, when we respond by faith to His revelation, we discover that God, indeed, speaks with truth and veracity in His revelation. He always performs what He has promised.

God has said He will meet our every need. Those of us who by faith have accepted that promise have discovered He does meet our needs.

Recently a student told me he and his wife had decided to pay cash for everything. They no longer planned to purchase on credit. The day after they made that decision, the brakes went out on their car. A mechanic told the student it would cost twenty dollars to repair the brakes. This was more money than the couple had. As a matter of fact, the couple had nothing on hand. They prayed about it and told God they were trusting Him to provide. The next day they received a check in the mail which was sufficient to cover the cost. Although the couple had not known where the money would come from when they prayed, they had discovered God was true to His promise to supply all their needs.

Although many do not believe in a standard of truth, men themselves prove God is a God of truth. The very fact that philosophers and others discuss what truth really is proves there is such a thing as truth. Whether they believe it or not, God is truth.

When the Lord Jesus was on trial before His crucifixion, Pontius Pilate asked Him, "What is truth?" What Pilate did not realize, of course, was that Jesus Christ was truth Himself. We know that truth is found only in God. We should be thankful that God has revealed Himself to us through His

Word because there we can truly come to know God and to know God is truth.

The truth of God is made known to us, first of all, in providing a revelation for us. It enables us to check up on the truthfulness or the veracity of God. One concept of truthfulness says that something must measure up to a standard. If the information is factual and correct; if there is no mistake in it; according to that concept, it is truth.

In His Word God tells us what He really is. On the basis of the revelation He has given of Himself we can come to some understanding of God. Then when we compare that standard to what He does and how He performs, we can tell He actually measures up to the standard He has established for Himself in His Word. God is exactly the kind of being that He has said He is.

Fulfillment of prophecy also demonstrates His truthfulness. This, too, comes out of the revelation of God's Word. God gave prophecies through men hundreds of years before they were fulfilled. Yet, when they were fulfilled, they were fulfilled in the minutest detail.

Some of the prophecies given in connection with the birth of our Lord Jesus Christ were given fifteen hundred years before the time of Christ. There is no way around it; the higher critics cannot escape the fact that these prophecies were fulfilled. They may date some of the books later, but there is no way they can date them after the time of Christ. The prophecies gave the tribe from which the Messiah was to come. They gave the place where He was to be born. They gave us His lineage in the finest detail. All of these fulfilled prophecies clearly indicate God is indeed a God of truthfulness.

We see God's faithfulness in connection with His covenants. God made covenants with men, some of which have been fulfilled. Others will yet be fulfilled. He made the covenants years before they were fulfilled. He told His people He would judge them if they were disobedient. True to His Word, He judged them when the time came.

The covenant God made with David is recorded in II Samuel 7. Some of the things He promised there were fulfilled when Christ was born. Others will be fulfilled in the future.

The New Testament speaks of a new covenant. Under this covenant God promised to deal with the problem of our sin. He dealt with the problem by sending His Son to die. On the basis of our faith in His Son, we become sons of God. Thus, He is faithful in fulfilling that covenant because, whenever anyone accepts Jesus Christ, his sins are forgiven and he becomes a new creature. The new covenant has once again been fulfilled.

When God promises He will fulfill. II Timothy 2:12, 13 says, "If we suffer, we shall also reign with him: if we deny him, he also will deny us: If we believe not, yet he abideth faithful; he cannot deny himself." Hebrews 6:17, 18; 10:23 also indicate that God abides faithful.

Finally, God's judgments demonstrate His faithfulness. In His Word God says He will judge His children. We know this happens for we have experienced judgment in our own lives. God judges us on whether or not we are dealing with sin in our lives. We have an advocate, Christ Jesus, with the Father. The Bible declares we can come and confess our sin and receive forgiveness (I John 1:9). However, if we do not confess our sin, Scripture clearly teaches us He will judge us. The judgment is always right; it is always adequate. He will not be unjust; nevertheless, He does judge us.

He also judges the lost. He may withhold judgment because of His mercy, but He will eventually judge. The day will come when those who have rejected Christ as Saviour will stand in the presence of Almighty God. That judgment will also be right and will manifest the truthfulness of God.

God's truthfulness should comfort us. Have you ever had someone promise to do something without fail only to find he has not kept his promise? You cannot really trust him after that. God is different. We can take comfort in the fact that we can depend on Him. When God says He will be with us in time of trouble, He will be there. When God says He will meet our need, He will meet our need. His truthfulness should give us assurance and give us a basis for our faith. You see, when God tells me if I put my faith in Jesus Christ, I am a child of God, I do become a child of God. On the basis of His Word, I have assurance that I am His child. I base my assurance upon His Word, not upon my feelings nor upon what someone else has said.

We can have this confidence:

If we receive the witness of men, the witness of God is greater: for this is the witness of God which he hath testified of his Son. He that believeth on the Son of God hath the witness in himself: he that believeth not God hath made him a liar; because he believeth not the record that God gave of his Son. And this is the record, that God hath given to us eternal life, and this life is in his Son. He that hath the Son hath life; and he that hath not the Son of God hath not life. These things have I written unto you that believe on the name of the Son of God; that ye may know that ye have eternal life, and that ye may believe on the name of the Son of God. (I John 5:9-13).

If this does not give us assurance for our faith, we are in effect saying God is not truthful. God is a liar. This we cannot do.

God's truthfulness is the basis for our hope and our rejoicing. My hope of one day being exactly like Jesus Christ is based upon the truthfulness of God. I rejoice because I know God will perform what He has said He will do. Therefore, His truthfulness leads me from despair.

Finally, as we appropriate the truth of God in the Word, and we actually see it being verified in our experience, His truthfulness should cause us to believe. It ought to help us believe even more the promises of God, to accept them and act upon them. It should cause us to want to be like Him. We ought to be known as men and women who are truthful. I believe this is what the Scripture means when it says, "let your nay be nay and your yea, yea."

We should not have to swear oaths to make people believe what we are saying. By our very nature people ought to know what we say is true. I resent someone asking me, "Are you really telling me the truth?" Of course I am because I am to manifest the nature of my God and He is a God of truthfulness. Such a God is worthy of our worship.

God's truthfulness has some implications for the unsaved as well. God says the unsaved will never stand in His presence as a sinner (Psalm 1:5). The only way the sinner can hope to stand before Him is to accept Jesus Christ. This is what God's Word says. He will stand by what He has said. May I encourage you even now to put your trust in Jesus Christ and, as you do so, you will discover that He is, indeed, a God of truthfulness.

13. His Patience

We think we know what patience is but the patience of God is different from the patience of men. Because Scripture says tribulation worketh patience, we generally tie patience in with suffering. We think a man is patient if in the face of suffering he just sort of bears it. This is not true of God. God's patience looks at His willingness to defer or withhold wrath. He holds judgment from men. He does not revenge Himself upon the world. He does not grieve when wrong occurs. It is true that God does not want men to sin, but God does not suffer anguish under those circumstances. He simply waits patiently to punish individuals according to their merits. He does not punish them immediately; He holds off their punishment.

We know from our discussion of the other attributes that God does have the power and the authority to punish immediately. However, because He has the characteristic of patience, He does not always choose to exercise that right. He waits to pour forth His judgment.

The patience of God is to some extent a part of the goodness of God. You remember, the goodness of God simply means God is willing to deal bountifully with His creatures. In one respect, the patience of God is based upon the goodness and mercy of God. Yet at the same time, the goodness of God and His mercy are not quite the same as His patience.

The mercy of God looks at the creature as miserable. He is in a bad state and God is merciful toward him. The patience of God looks upon man as a criminal, as one who is worthy only of punishment. Mercy pities the creature. Patience bears with the creature. Mercy may lead to patience because God is merciful; He withholds His judgment and thus He exercises His patience. Yet, the two are not the same. Patience also glorifies the grace of God in the case of the child of God. The very fact that God is patient with us as His children is simply an example of His grace. We also see His patience when He is gracious toward us by withholding His judgment.

Although man is the primary object of God's patience, some of God's other creation, such as animals and nature, also benefit from His patience. For example, God withholds judgment from the earth and from the animals because of His patience in waiting to judge men.

God is patient even though He knows all things. On the other hand, because we do not know the whole situation, we are sometimes impatient with other people.

Recently a student came to class a bit late. By the time he arrived, I had already picked up the assigned papers from the other students.

To his consternation, when he opened his notebook to take out his paper, he found only the last page. Startled, he said, "Oh, I thought I had all the pages in here but I've only got the last page. May I put it in your mailbox as soon as class is over?"

"OK," I told him, demonstrating my patience. "Put a note on it."

At noon I went to my box but the paper was not there. At this point, I merely supposed the student had handed it in and the girls at the desk had not yet put it in my box. About five o'clock, before I went home, I checked again and found the paper was in my box. As a result, I assumed the student had told me the truth, and I believe he did.

It is possible, however, and this is for illustration only, that he did not have the paper done after all. He may have had it partially finished and have done the remainder after class. (However, normally a person would start at the beginning of the paper and not at the end, but I had no way of knowing whether he actually had the last page.) If I had known all the details in respect to what had happened I might not have exhibited the patience that I did. But God knows everything. Yet, He is patient. He knows whether or not we sin deliberately. Even then, He is still patient with us and waits for us to confess our sin of our own will.

God also has the power to revenge Himself upon men, but He does not always use it. Let me emphasize that the patience of God is not cowardice on His part, nor is it lack of ability or right on the part of God. God does have the power to do what He desires to do, but His patience says that He does not exercise that right or privilege which is His by virtue of His being God. God has control over all His creatures but He also has control over Himself. Therefore He can wait patiently.

Have you discovered that sometimes you do not have complete control over yourself? I grew up on a farm, and in the wintertime most of our living was done in one room because we heated only one room. One cold day during Christmas vacation, after we had done our chores, my brother and I sat on the floor and bounced a ball back and forth across the room. We soon found out it was getting on my mother's nerves.

"Will you please stop bouncing that ball?" she finally said.

We stopped bouncing it and we began to roll it. However, we soon tired of rolling it because it was not exciting enough. We began to bounce it again. Maybe we did it deliberately. Eventually my mother lost control; her patience gave way and we caught it. The ball disappeared.

God is not like that. He never loses control of Himself. He exercises His patience as long as He desires to exercise it. I wish I could say that of myself.

Be aware also that God's patience does not conflict with God's holiness or His truthfulness or His justice or any other characteristic. God simply waits. Ultimately, all His other attributes will be completely satisfied.

What proof do we have of God's patience? Nahum 1:3 says, "The Lord is slow to anger, and great in power, and will not at all acquit the wicked.''

God's patience is demonstrated by His preserving creation. When Adam and Eve sinned, God could just as well have said, ''I've had it. I'm going to blot out the whole thing and start over again.''

God did not do that. He continued to manifest His patience by preserving His creation. Ultimately, of course, He will change creation so it will once again be like it was originally.

The patience of God also shows His care for man. I really do not understand why God does some of the things He does. I am glad He does, but I do not understand it. I do not understand why He is so patient with men. It seems it would be much easier for Him if He would simply take men off the earth when He saves them. Instead, He leaves us here and He is so patient with us, His children. When we fail Him time after time, He patiently bears with us. His Holy Spirit works with us to make us aware of our sin. He patiently cares for men. He meets our every need even though we have failed Him time after time. He is patient.

When Adam and Eve sinned, God took them out of the Garden of Eden so they could not eat of the Tree of Life and thus live forever in their fallen state. He gave them opportunity to come to a better understanding of Himself. Adam and Eve did learn some things about God that they evidently did not know prior to the fall.

The children of Israel remained in Egypt as long as they did because of the patience of God. He waited over four hundred years to judge the

Amorites before their cup of iniquity was filled in the Land of Promise. At the end of His patience, God brought the children of Israel out of Egypt and used them to judge the Amorites.

Because God's patience had been exhausted, He instructed the Israelites to destroy the Amorites. It does not mean, however, that God had no more patience. It simply meant that He had reached the place where He felt there was no more profit in His being patient with the Amorites.

The Old Testament records that the children of Israel failed repeatedly, but God exercised His patience toward His people repeatedly.

As the cycles in the Book of Judges illustrate some of God's other attributes, they also illustrate His patience. Israel would fall into sin and an oppressing nation would judge them. In agony, Israel would call out to God. God, in turn, would forgive them and relieve them of their oppression. Israel would enjoy peace for a period of time but once again they would drift into sin, and apostasy would come upon them.

Although they followed this cycle seven times in the Book of Judges, God very patiently restored them, then blessed them. The same pattern repeats itself when the kings ruled. Most of the kings—who, by the way, came directly from their people—were bad, but God patiently waited, until finally in II Kings 17, Assyria took the northern kingdom captive. God was free to judge them long before this incident, but He withheld judgment until then.

God is also very patient toward the Gentiles. God

has given the Gentiles a couple of thousand years to have dominion over His people, Israel. Nevertheless, judgment will come. God's chosen race has suffered intensely at the hand of the Gentiles. We saw this particularly during the persecution which occurred during World War II. God is patiently waiting, giving the Gentiles ample opportunity to repent. Nevertheless, the day will come when His judgment will fall upon Gentile nations.

Even when judgment comes, God demonstrates His patience. He brings only enough judgment to bear to make us aware of our sin. He is very, very patient. He gives us opportunity to repent, and if we do not repent, He judges only as needed. He could immediately take us in physical death. But He does not. In contrast, when we judge we have a tendency to not only deliver *adequate* judgment, but we go beyond and punish over and above what is fair and equitable.

Why is God patient? God wants to show us that we can appease Him. He is not an implacable enemy. We can approach Him. We can come into His presence. If God were to smite us down every time we did something that displeased Him, we would think of Him as our enemy. However, God is not our enemy; He is our friend. He wants us to repent of our own free will. He does not want to force us. He wants us to become aware of our sin and willingly confess it, thus receiving forgiveness.

Parents want this of their children, as well. It is not difficult to tell when a child has been disobedient. When our children were small, I tried to withhold action to give the child a chance to come to me first. I felt it was better for him to come to me and say, "Dad, I did something that I know you're not going to like, but I feel I have to tell you about it. This is what I did; will you forgive me?"

Personally, I think this is a much better approach than for me to call in the child and say, "Look, this is what you've done. Are you going to deal with it?" Obviously, that puts it on an altogether different basis. God also wants us to come to Him of our own free will.

If God were not patient, the human race would cease to exist. Not only would the human race cease to exist, but the church would no longer continue. I don't know about you, but on occasion I have just a little bit of a problem with sin. If He were to judge me and every other Christian immediately and take us home as He really ought, then obviously, the church would cease to exist. Now, some of you might last longer than I, but I don't think you'd last too long either. Continuing to sin is not a rationale for demonstrating the patience of God, but it is the rationale for the church continuing to exist. The church is made up of individuals who continue to sin. We ought not to abuse the patience of God. I am afraid we take advantage of His patience far too often.

What should the patience of God do for us? As with the other attributes, it ought to cause us to worship God. Is there anything else we can do when we think of His patience in light of His other attributes, particularly in light of His authority, His dominion

134

and His holiness? We fall short of His righteousness and we deserve judgment. However, He is patient.

Furthermore, His patience ought to comfort us. If He is so gracious and patient with His enemies, what will He do for those who are striving to please Him? If God will patiently wait for a sinner to accept Jesus Christ as Saviour so He can bestow grace upon him, what will He do for that individual when the individual becomes God's child? Obviously He will continue to be patient. He will continue to be gracious. Even more so. This ought to comfort us. It should cause us to trust His promises. It should comfort us in our weakness. It should not be a cause for sinning, but when we sin we should take advantage of His forgiveness.

We ought to meditate upon the patience of God. If we do, it will lead us to repentance. It will cause us to resent in others the things they are doing which bring injury to our God. We ought to point out to sinning Christians, particularly, that they cannot put God's patience to a test indefinitely. They need to recognize that God will ultimately judge. We ought to help them see their need.

Above all, we ought to imitate the patience of God. Certainly, God is willing to help us with this. We ought to ask the Holy Spirit to help us be patient people. We ought not to judge others on the spur of the moment, but we ought to wait and give them opportunity to repent as God does us. We have a patient God.

135

14. His Jealousy

Many believe God cannot be a jealous God because jealousy is sin. However, the Scriptures clearly teach that God is a jealous God just as they teach God is a God of wrath. Exodus 20:3-6 says:

Thou shalt have no other gods before me. Thou shalt not make unto thee any graven [carved] image, or any likeness of any thing that is in heaven above, or that is in the earth beneath, or that is in the water under the earth: Thou shalt not bow down thyself to them, nor serve them; for I the Lord thy God am a jealous God, visiting the iniquity of the fathers upon the children unto the third and fourth generation of them that hate me. And shewing mercy unto thousands of them that love me, and keep my commandments.

In Exodus 34, God says His people are to be a holy people and if they obey His commands, He will drive the Amorites and Canaanites out of the land, and He will go before them. In verse 14 He says, "For thou shalt worship no other god; for the Lord, whose name is Jealous, is a jealous God."

Contrary to what we believe, jealousy is not necessarily sinful. When Scripture says God is a jealous God, God is using a term which we will understand. This is called an anthropomorphism. To us, jealousy is sin. Our concept of someone who is jealous is someone who is coveting something that does not belong to him. Our jealousy is usually a result of envy or perhaps even spite, but this is not true of God. God does not covet. Actually, in God, jealousy is something that is correct. It is a proper attitude. It is a correct response on His part. As a matter of fact, jealousy can also be a correct response on our part.

The dictionary defines jealousy as "a solicitous care to defend one's honor, one's right and so forth. It is an awareness of one's rightful position in the life of another, and the desire to keep or preserve one's position."

This is how God feels about us. God says, "I am the One who should hold your full allegiance. You are to be loyal to Me. You are to be concerned about Me. If anyone tries to take My place or if you give it to anyone else, then I am jealous."

God also had a right to first place in the lives of the children of Israel. After all, God had delivered them out of Egypt. When He gave the Ten Commandments, He was about to give them the Promised Land. He had every right to claim their allegiance and their loyalty. He had a right to first place in their affections, in their lives and in their worship. God did not sin when He became jealous because they gave that position to someone else.

Jealousy can be based upon covetousness or even maliciousness. In man, jealousy may well lead to a spiteful action. In human beings it often stems from and is fed by pride. Because we are proud we do not want anyone else to assume the position that we think is ours. Jealousy can be misappropriation of a relationship to another person.

Recently in our city, police arrested a man for shooting his former lover and her date. According to the newspaper, he felt the girl still belonged to him and that the man who was now dating her was assuming his rightful place. His was an improper response. The man was jealous because of hurt pride. Although he thought someone was taking something that belonged to him, the girl did not think so.

God is not that way. God does not become jealous simply because His pride is injured. God does not become jealous because He covets something that someone else has. God is jealous because someone attempts to take His rightful position, the place that belongs to Him.

Regardless of present-day standards, the husband and wife relationship is an exclusive one. Any second lover, whether a man or a woman, who enters into that relationship should produce jealousy on the part of the spouse, the one who is being replaced. Such reaction is perfectly legitimate and is not sinful.

On the other hand, if the jealousy leads the marriage partner who has been wronged into actions of force and violence, sin occurs, but the jealousy in itself is not the sin. If the individual is not jealous, it indicates that the marriage already is faulty.

When the Bible says God is a jealous God, it means He demands complete faithfulness and loyalty from those whom He has loved and redeemed. God is not jealous with respect to the person outside of Jesus Christ. His jealousy is with respect to the saved because we have responded to His love and we say we have put Him first in our lives. He is our God and therefore He demands complete faithfulness and loyalty. When we allow any other being or any other thing to take that place of preeminence, God is rightfully jealous.

God will vindicate His claim by judging those who place someone else or some other thing in His rightful position. His vindication of His claim illustrates the wrath of God. Because God is jealous, He will claim His rightful position in the lives of His own and this may lead to an outpouring of His wrath upon them.

Do we have proof of the jealousy of God? I have already referred to one passage of Scripture, but we have many other references that state God is jealous. See Deuteronomy 4:24; 6:15; 29:20; 32:16,21. Joshua, I and II Kings, Ezekiel, Joel and Zechariah also contain passages which say God is jealous. First Corinthians 10:22 and James 4:5 in the New Testament also confirm His jealousy.

Not only do the Scriptures support God's jealousy, but His actions demonstrate that He is jealous. Whenever the child of God gives anything or any being God's rightful place, God acts. God has made a covenant with His people just as we in our marriage make a covenant with one another, and any violation of our vows produces jealousy.

The same was true with the children of Israel. When they worshiped idols, God judged them. When they made treaties with other nations, God judged them. When they intermarried with pagan people, God judged them.

The Old Testament looks upon the people of God as being in a covenant relationship with Him. The writers of the Old Testament often set forth this covenant relationship in terms of marriage. They said, for example, that God took Israel as His bride. Therefore, when someone took God's rightful place in that marriage, that person committed adultery. When Israel turned to idols, God looked upon it as breaking the marriage bond—spiritual adultery— and God became jealous. So He judged them. However, God always restored Israel when they repented.

Why is God jealous? God is jealous because He loves us. God has entered into a permanent relationship with us. If He did not love us He would not be jealous. The very fact that God says He is jealous indicates His love for us. It indicates that He is concerned about us and wants us to be in our proper relationship with Him.

We read in Ezekiel 39:25 that God is jealous for His holy name. He does not want us to put anything in His rightful place. Most of us do not have carved images in our lives, but we are apt to put our cars, our homes or our businesses first in our affections. To do so is to commit sin. He does not want sin in the life of the believer. We are to be a holy people. If we do anything that detracts from God's place in our lives, in our affections and in our loyalty, it is sin.

In Isaiah 42:8 and 48:11, God says He will not give His glory to another. Because of this, He is jealous of anyone who assumes that position of glory in our lives. If anyone usurps His place of glory, God is jealous.

What does this mean to us? God's jealousy demonstrates that God loves us. He does not want anyone to replace Him. Almighty God, the kind of God about which we have been talking, is so concerned about His relationship with us that He will do anything to protect and preserve that relationship. It ought to make us sensitive to the will of God. It should make us zealous for the Lord.

God's deepest wish for us is for Him to have first place in our lives. This knowledge should cause us to do all we can to please Him, and to avoid sin in any form. The moment that we become aware that we are putting someone or something in God's rightful place, we ought to deal with it. It provokes God to jealousy. His jealousy may lead to wrath and to judgment.

We ought to be aware of this in the lives of others. If we understand the jealousy of God, we should try to help other believers give God His rightful position. This is difficult because most of us do not like to become involved in the problems of others.

We ought to encourage the whole body of Christ to be zealous for God. In Revelation 3:15-19, God reprimanded the church at Laodicea for their lack of zeal. "I know thy works, that thou art neither cold nor hot: I would thou wert cold or hot. So then because thou art lukewarm, and neither cold nor hot, I will spue [spew] thee out of my mouth" (verses 15,16).

God wants us to be "all out" for Him. He actually would almost rather have us be against Him than just in the middle—no interest one way or another. God says, "As many as I love I rebuke and chasten. Be zealous therefore and repent."

We as a people of God ought to be zealous for God because we recognize that God is jealous. If anything comes into the life of the church as a corporate body of believers that replaces God, He will judge us.

Above all, we should examine our own lives. God's jealousy should assure us that God loves us and is concerned about our relationship with Him. The very fact that He is jealous indicates He knows we belong to Him.

It should also comfort us for we know that God will forgive and restore if we repent.

God's jealousy should cause us to worship and praise our God because He is indeed this kind of God. He demands first place and He rightfully deserves it because He is indeed the Lord Almighty. We ought to worship and praise Him.

Does God have any reason to be jealous of your life? Does God have His rightful place in your life?

15. His Wrath

Many feel it is not right to talk about the wrath of God. They feel that a perfect God cannot be a God of wrath. The problem with this reasoning is that we look upon wrath from our point of view. Our wrath on many occasions is improper and for us it is sin. This not true of God.

According to the dictionary, wrath is deep, intense anger and indignation. Anger is usually thought to be the result of injury or insult. Indignation is generally looked upon as righteous anger aroused by injustice.

Most of us probably sin when we become angry because our anger usually comes as a result of our impotence. We find ourselves unable to act in the way we want to and therefore we become angry. It is an indication of our weakness, our impotence.

Of course, God does not react with anger in such situations because He has the power to act. God is all-powerful; He not only has the right to do what He wants, but He has the ability. Therefore, He never reacts because He is unable to perform. God reacts because there is an injury or insult aimed at Him. He does not react because He has been thwarted. God never sins when He is angry.

The church today does not emphasize this. When was the last time you heard a sermon on the wrath of God? Today, we tend to emphasize the love of God. It is true, God is a God of love, but we will never fully understand the love of God nor appreciate His mercy and grace unless we consider the wrath of God. As a matter of fact, there are more references in Scripture which refer to God's wrath than there are which refer to God's love. We tend to emphasize what is favorable or good. We do not emphasize the unpleasant. To emphasize the love of God, His goodness and mercy and grace is not all bad, but if we neglect the wrath of God, we lack balance. The wrath of God is an extremely important truth in the Word of God. Ministers who neglect to teach it sin not only against God but against the people to whom they minister.

When I took a course in American literature in college, the famous sermon by Jonathan Edwards was one of the required pieces of literature. Preached in colonial days, that sermon helped spark the "Great Awakening" in the United States. Edwards described God as a God of wrath to his audiences. He drew word pictures of sinners dangling over the pits of hell. Those in his congregation became so frightened that they hid under the pews. My professor told the class this was not a proper representation of God. He poked fun at Edwards and his message.

"God cannot be that kind of God," my professor said. He was wrong. God is a God of wrath. Scripture declares it. God emphasizes that fact because we have a tendency to overlook that characteristic, and He wants us to realize we must answer for our sin. Because God is holy, He hates sin and His wrath must be poured out upon us.

The wrath of God is not a popular subject. Many feel wrath would be a blot on God's character. For the most part, when we become angry, we give way to wrath. Our wrath is sin because the cause for our anger is improper. However, God is holy and He hates sin. Because He is just, He must judge sin. That means He must pour His wrath upon sinful people. We cannot escape. God is a God of wrath.

Do we have proof of His wrath? Isaiah 63:1-6 vividly portrays His wrath:

Who is this that cometh from Edom, with dyed garments from Bozrah? this that is glorious in his apparel, travelling in the greatness of his strength? I that speak in righteousness, mighty to save. Wherefore art thou red in thine apparel, and thy garments like him that treadeth in the winefat? I have trodden the winepress alone; and of the people there was none with me: for I will tread them in mine anger, and trample them in my fury; and their blood shall be sprinkled upon my garments, and I will stain all my raiment. For the day of vengeance is in mine heart, and the year of my redeemed is come. And I looked, and there was none to help; and I wondered that there was none to uphold: therefore mine own arm brought salvation unto me; and my fury, it upheld me. And I

will tread down the people in mine anger, and
make them drunk in my fury, and I will bring
down their strength to the earth.

Here God is administering final judgment upon
the people for their treatment of His people, Israel.
He is pouring out His judgment because of what
they have done to His chosen race. We see it in the
Psalms on many occasions. Some critics say these
Psalms are not really worthy of God because the
psalmist cries out that God will wreak vengeance
upon the psalmist's enemies. The writer of the
Psalms is perfectly free to do this because God says
He will judge His enemies, that He will pour out His
wrath upon them. If God is going to do that to His
enemies, then certainly the psalmist who is walking
with God should be able to ask God to judge his
human enemies and take care of them. We also see
God's wrath in Deuteronomy 2.

This is not just a characteristic of God shown in
the Old Testament, but it is also shown in the New.
It is clearly set forth in the Book of Romans. As a
matter of fact, Jesus Christ talked a great deal about
the wrath of God. On one occasion, He said it was
better for an individual to maim himself than to face
the wrath of God and the lake of fire. Thus, we see
Christ Himself acknowledging that God will pour
out His wrath upon sinners.

Romans 1:18,19 says, "For the wrath of God is
revealed from heaven against all ungodliness and
unrighteousness of men, who hold the truth in
unrighteousness." Paul, the writer, goes on to give

the reason. "Because that which may be known of God is manifest in them; for God hath shewed [shown] it unto them."

You see, God has a reason for pouring out His wrath upon men. He has a proper basis for being angry because He has revealed Himself unto men and men have rejected that revelation. God does not arbitrarily pour out His wrath. He does it because men have rejected the light that He has given to them. As a result, judgment comes.

On a few occasions in Scripture God actually swears an oath; that is, He actually takes an oath that something will be true. In Psalm 89:35, He swears by His holiness and in Psalm 95:11 He swears in His wrath. In the second reference God says, "Unto whom I sware in my wrath that they should not enter into my rest." In this case, He swore because of His wrath, His judgment that was to be poured out upon the children of Israel. The children of Israel did not enter into rest. The setting of this Psalm was the Wilderness where the children of Israel were wandering on their way to the Promised Land. Because of their disobedience and refusal to believe the revelation God had given them, God swore in His wrath they would not enter the Promised Land. That whole generation, twenty years of age and upward, died in the Wilderness as a result of their unbelief. Once again, God's wrath came in response to the actions of men. God's wrath is also seen immediately after Adam and Eve sinned. Adam and Eve failed to meet the responsibility God had given them, and therefore God judged them. He

147

drove them out of the Garden of Eden and they could not come back.

Later in the Book of Genesis, we see God's judgment on Cain when he murdered his brother. In chapters six through nine, we see God's judgment falling on the whole of mankind as He sends the Flood to judge the terrible sin of the people who turned their back on God.

Remember, God is not arbitrary in His wrath. He does not react with a fit of rage or spite because He has been thwarted; He simply pronounces judgment on man's sin because He is holy, righteous and just.

The wrath of God is manifested in the way in which the world operates. The world was also affected by Adam and Eve's sin. In Romans 8:22, we read that the world was judged when Adam and Eve were judged. Therefore, the wrath of God was poured upon the whole world as a result of Adam and Eve's sin. The verse says, "For we know that the whole creation groaneth and travaileth in pain together until now." According to the early chapters of Genesis, men now have problems with weeds, thistles, thorns and briars because of the judgment of God. God poured out His wrath upon the world because the world was affected by sin.

God also shows His wrath by judging sinners in the Old Testament. However, He judged not only those unrighteous individuals who we might say rightly deserved judgment, but He judged His own people. Even Moses, the leader who took the children of Israel out of Egypt toward the Promised Land, was judged. He had faithfully followed God's guidance all those years until they were ready to enter the land. There was little water and the people murmured and complained. God told Moses to speak to the rock to produce water. However, Moses, in his anger, smote the rock and God judged him.

God said to Moses, "Because you have sinned, because you became angry when the children of Israel murmured and complained, you will not be allowed to go into the Land of Promise." Perhaps this was not the most severe judgment but at least it indicates that God metes out wrath upon His children.

God also judged the children of Israel when Achan sinned (Joshua 7). After the fall of Jericho, Achan took garments, gold and silver and hid them in his tent. Because of Achan's sin, God caused Ai to defeat Israel. So we see God did not spare righteous individuals of the Old Testament any more than He did the unrighteous.

We clearly see the wrath of God when we view the life of the Lord Jesus Christ, and particularly when we view His death on the cross. We need to understand that God in His wrath is judging sin. When we see how God pours out His wrath upon His only Son, it should cause us to understand what sin really means to God. It clearly indicates the seriousness of sin and God's hatred for it. Because of His hatred for sin, God must punish it. Christ died so that the wrath of God might be satisfied against the sinner, so he can receive forgiveness.

We ought also to realize that God is not through

yet. He will still exercise His wrath in time to come. In Isaiah 63 we see a description of some of the events which will occur when God wraps up all things. Then, He will ultimately deal with sin. The Book of Revelation indicates that God will pour out His wrath upon mankind in one judgment after another. Literally millions of people will die because of His judgment. Some of the plagues that are coming are going to take a third of the earth's population in one wave. Famine, destruction, warfare, pestilence, unnatural events are going to occur and God's wrath will be seen as never before. That will be a great and terrible time.

What should we learn from God's wrath? We ought to understand that God is no less perfect just because He is a God of wrath. God can be perfectly holy and yet demonstrate His wrath against sin.

We ought to let the world know that God will deal with sin. Deep down, the world knows God will punish sin, that He will pour out His wrath upon sin. Nevertheless, the people of the world try to ignore it.

We need to meditate upon the wrath of God. Scripture says we ought to think about all the perfections of God. We cannot consider God's total personality and leave out His wrath. We ought to avoid sin because God will judge us. The writer of the Book of Hebrews says the fear of God ought to motivate us to live godly lives. We should think about the wrath of God; it will help us do the will of God.

The wrath of God ought to comfort us because it indicates that God will indeed judge sin. Sometimes we assume that sin will not be judged, but it will. On the basis of Deuteronomy 32:43 and Revelation 19:1,2 God will judge sin; there is no question about it. Not only will He judge our sin, but He will also judge the sins of all people. This judgment is particularly described in the nineteenth and twentieth chapters of Revelation. Judgment is sure.

Finally, the wrath of God should cause us to more fully appreciate what God has done for us in Jesus Christ. Because of His death, we do not have to face the wrath of a holy, righteous, just God. That wrath has been poured out upon the Lord Jesus Christ. We will never fully understand the love, the mercy and the grace of God until we put it against the backdrop of the wrath of God.

Again, this is what happened when the "Great Awakening" took place. When Jonathan Edwards, George Whitefield and others preached the wrath of God, men became aware of a God who judged sin, and they responded to the message of God's love. This is exactly what an emphasis on God's wrath should do for us. It ought to make us aware that God will judge sin. It should make us stop and think.

The wrath of God should cause sinners to stop and think as well. They should recognize that if they turn to God in faith, they will experience God's love and fully understand and appreciate that love. If the wrath of God is not emphasized, the love of God becomes a sentimental, meaningless nothing. It then can only mean that people can do what they want with impunity because God in some way will ultimately accept them. There is no scriptural basis for this. Sin must be judged. Either it is judged in the Person of Jesus Christ or else the individual will have to stand and bear the wrath of God by himself.

The Book of Revelation tells us that great and mighty men will cry out for the rocks and mountains to fall upon them and hide them from the wrath of God. It is not going to be an easy thing to stand in the presence of the Almighty God, the One who has all power, the One who has the right to do all that He wishes. He has all power, all authority and He pours out His wrath upon sinful man. The sinner needs to flee to the Lord Jesus Christ and be saved. Our God is a God of wrath.

16. Our Response— Worship

After considering the greatness of our God, there can be only one response—worship. What is worship?

Recently while spending a few days in Colorado, we hiked up one of the mountains. We stood at the top and looked out over the tree-covered peaks surrounding us. My chest tightened as I looked at the "purple majesty" stretched before me and I knew how Frances Bates must have felt when she wrote the lyrics to the song, "America." We may think of this as worship, and yet, although I was moved, merely thinking of the beauty did not constitute worship. However, as we stood there, someone suggested we sing the song, "God is so Great." As we sang several verses of the song, my soul reached out to God, the mighty Creator. Later we united in prayer. That was worship.

Worship can be demonstrated in other ways as well. Many of us think sitting in a church sanctuary, listening to an organ prelude is an act of worship. Yet, simply to be there and to listen is not an act of worship. Listening to music may give us pleasure but that is not worship. It may help us in our act of worship, but unless we respond to God, it is not worship.

Worship is the response of the creature to the Eternal God. It is an acknowledgment of His transcendence. That is, there is a reality that is independent of the worshiper, which is colored by mystery. We do not really understand that reality but we know that that personality outside of ourselves was there first. Worship, then, is an acknowledgment of His transcendence and a reality which exists outside and beyond ourselves.

Worship must include an awareness of God and a consideration of Him. We must think about Him, not merely listen to music or admire nature. Our minds must be focused on God.

Sometimes man worships other things, but worship belongs to God and God alone. We may worship the creation of our hands. We may worship another person, but none of these are truly worship, for worship is the response of the creature to the Eternal.

Actually, men have a need to worship. When God made mankind, He put in man the need to worship Him. We do not always recognize that need and, consequently, we do not always worship God as we ought. We see this particularly among pagan peoples in their worship of physical idols. They make an image which fits their concept of God. They bow down to that image and worship it. This, of course, is an act of worship which should be directed to the eternal God. However, the fact that men in all cultures do worship something is an indication that God made man with a need to offer worship to a higher being. Man has prostituted that worship; yet, the need is there.

According to John 4, God is a spirit. In that passage of Scripture Christ said, "God is a Spirit: and they that worship him must worship him in spirit and in truth" (John 4:24). God is a spiritual being and as such we should worship Him. We generally recognize spiritual beings as being supernatural. That is, they are different from men and so we recognize them as being greater and as having more power. Therefore, the very fact that God is a spiritual being indicates His superiority to us and we ought to worship Him because of this.

Above and beyond that, we ought to worship Him simply because of what He is. He is God. He is a good God. He is an unchangeable God. He is a God of love, mercy and grace. He is a holy, righteous, just and merciful God. All of the characteristics we have discussed are true of our God. Therefore, we ought to love and honor Him. We ought to think about Him. We ought to revere Him. We ought to worship Him because He is a spirit and because of all that He is.

Although we have a need to worship, we cannot know how or whom to worship from nature. Looking at nature may motivate us to say, "My, this is really beautiful. This is tremendous. It must be something special that brought this into being." However, we only know whom we should worship or how we should worship from God's revelation or self-disclosure. Scripture tells us whom we are to worship. We are to offer our worship to God alone.

His Word also tells us what worship involves. Worship always has been an obligation for men to fulfill because worship is founded upon the very nature of God Himself.

A rather simple definition of worship defines it as concern about the Person and work of God. It means to meditate, to think about, to contemplate on Who and What He is. Worship is not so much a response to *what He has done* but a response to *what He is.* It means to revere, to meditate on the perfection of our God. Therefore, simply because God has created us, because of the very nature of God, worship has been and always will be our obligation to fulfill.

It is man's duty to worship God. God is the One whom we are to worship, and to offer that worship to anyone else is to deny the very being of God Himself. By worshiping something or someone other than God, we are implying that thing is worthy of worship and that God is not or that He does not even exist.

We can use our total beings in worship. We worship God not only in thinking about Him, but we can sing as an act of worship of God. To make singing an act of worship necessitates a song that deals with the Person of God and His perfections. For example, when we sing the hymn, "Holy, Holy, Holy," we are singing a hymn of worship. We are concentrating upon His attribute of holiness. It is an act of worship.

We can also worship in our prayer time; however, the act of worship does not involve petition or intercession. It is an act of prayer which simply concentrates on the perfections of our God. We thank Him for Who and What He is. We pour out our hearts in praise, worship and adoration simply because God is God.

When I think of my own prayer life and when I listen to the public prayers of others, I am convinced that our prayer life does not include enough worship. I believe part of the time spent in personal devotions should involve simple contemplation of God and His perfection. When was the last time you spent time just thinking about the fact that God is an unchanging God? When is the last time you have thought about the fact that God is a God of mercy and His mercy is new and fresh every morning? We ought to meditate upon the nature and being of our God. When we do this, we are worshiping.

A contemplation of God and all that He is will also lead us to be obedient and to do that which He desires. Doing the will of God, I believe, can actually be an act of worship, for it demonstrates that God is indeed God.

What then is spiritual worship? Spiritual worship is the act of understanding the excellency of God, seeing the glory of His attributes and recognizing Him as the Lord, governor of the world and, of course, of us as well. Spiritual worship is simply understanding the perfections of our God, meditating upon them or singing about them. It is concentrating upon Who and What He is.

If it is to be spiritual, worship must be offered from a person who is a spiritual being. According to

Scripture, man was originally a spiritual being; he had intimate fellowship with God. The Book of Genesis says God sought fellowship with mankind in the cool of the evening. Then sin entered and the fellowship was broken. Man became alienated from God. His spirit was looked upon as dead.

If we are to offer spiritual worship to God, we must be spiritual beings. According to the Scriptures, the only way we can become spiritual beings and offer the kind of worship we read about in John 4 is to become sons of God. This, of course, is done through faith in Jesus Christ. When we accept Jesus Christ, we are regenerated by the Spirit of God. We become spiritual beings. Therefore, once we are in fellowship with God through faith in Christ, we can offer spiritual worship. We can worship God wherever we are because we worship God spiritually.

The Spirit of God will assist our worship. Romans 8:26 says the Holy Spirit intercedes for us with "groanings which cannot be uttered." When we are contemplating the person of our God, all of His attributes and excellencies, it is difficult for us to understand because He is infinite and we are finite. It is impossible for us to truly understand all that our God is; however, the Holy Spirit, without our even necessarily being aware of it, enables us to worship God spiritually. He, in effect, expresses to God an understanding of God of which we are incapable.

Furthermore, if our worship is to be spiritual, it will be done from proper motivation. Both Cain and Abel were performing acts of worship to God. Abel was accepted; Cain was rejected. Why? Cain was improperly motivated. I do not think it would have made a bit of difference in God's response to Cain if he had brought a blood sacrifice. You see, the value of the sacrifice was not merely in the blood itself, but in the proper motive. Unless Cain had changed his attitude, God would not have accepted him even if he had brought a blood sacrifice.

This is also seen in the New Testament in the case of the Pharisee and the publican. Both men approached God on the basis of a sacrifice. The Pharisee said, "I thank God that I am not like this other man. I fast and I do this, and I do this." He was proud of his own works, and he was motivated not because of a desire for fellowship, but because of a desire for man's praise. The publican simply said, "God, be merciful to me a sinner." He recognized that he was guilty of sin and worthy of death. He recognized the holiness and the justice of God. He knew that coming into the presence of that kind of a being required some form of atonement. So, as an act of worship, He came and was accepted.

Is worship an idle act on our part? Worshiping God should make us aware of our relationship with Him. It implies we are His children. We know Him. We know something about Him. Not much, but we know *something* about Him. We come as children of God and when we contemplate God, we come to know ourselves better because we realize how different we are from Him. However, if we are children of God, there ought to be some resemblance between us and God. In an act of worship we come to a better and deeper understanding of God. We learn about Him.

One of the most profitable studies for me personally in my nearly thirty years of Bible teaching has been this study of the attributes of God. This is because I now know something about Him that I did not know before. I admit that I do not know much, but I know more than I did before. I know something of the kind of being He is. I know that He is a good God, a holy, a righteous and a just God. I know that more fully than I knew before. In the same way, worship should bring us to a deeper understanding of our God.

It should comfort us to know that any act of worship, the minutest act of worship, is acceptable to our God because He is gracious and will accept our acts of worship—insignificant though they may be.

It should also lead us to exhort one another. Refusal to worship God is sin. We should be concerned about our worship. We ought to ask one another whether or not we actually worship God or whether we forget all about Him. Are we so concerned about our needs and the needs of others that we neglect to worship? We ought to worship God because He alone is worthy of all worship. Our God is a great God. He is worthy of our worship.